Mary Woster Haug offers a lovely, ruminative book transcending usual boundaries of memoir and travel writing. Set in modern, bustling Korea during a teaching year abroad, but forever grounded within memories from South Dakota's stark landscape, Haug's writing evokes the intoxications of boiled silkworm, blood sausage, and Korean *kimchi*. These appear amid wafting tugs of childhood illness, a sometimes overanxious mother, and the magic of a childhood in Lakota country. At a marketplace kiosk in Daejeon city, the author shows us the ancient art of Korean knot-tying, how to fashion a *maedeup*, wherein "the weaver controls each step from teasing out the silk strands, intertwining them into a single *sul*, and then braiding them into a knot: a double-cinch knot that braids two separate strands into a *maedeup* that grows stronger with each tug." Such intricate artistry, dating back some twenty-two centuries in Korea, fashions Haug's own book where knots of writer observation and memory grow all the stronger for our efforts to unravel them.

I am transfixed by her intimate writing of a bashful visit to a Korean spa which is frequented without shame by naked women young and old. "I came to understand that scrubbing an old woman's back is an act of generosity," she writes, then knots this moment into the ever-tightening vision of her own mother, naked and defeated, in a nursing home near the end of her life. She asks, "Would she instinctively recoil at someone touching her naked flesh? Or would she relax into my hands scrubbing her back with a soft cloth?" Such honest questions will not easily free readers inevitably snared by the intricately braided *maedeup* of *Daughters of the Grasslands*.

—Daniel W. Lehman, co-editor of *River Teeth: A Journal of Nonfiction Narrative*; author of *Matters of Fact: Reading Nonfiction Over the Edge*

BOTTOM DOG PRESS

Daughters
of the Grasslands

Through the
Looking Glass of Korea

A Memoir

Mary Woster Haug

Harmony Memoir Series
Bottom Dog Press
Huron, Ohio

ISBN 978-1-93396492-8

Bottom Dog Publishing
PO Box 425, Huron, Ohio 44839
http://smithdocs.net
e-mail: Lsmithdog@smithdocs.net

General Editor: Larry Smith
Editor, Layout & Cover Design: Susanna Sharp-Schwacke
Copy Editor: Devlin Geroski
Interior Author Photo: South Dakota State University
Marketing and Communication

ACKNOWLEDGMENTS

Dr. Peggy Elliot Miller provided generous financial
support. Kathy Murphy, the Benedictine Sisters at the Peace
Center in Yankton, and Linda Hasselstrom at Windbreak
House in Hermosa offered quiet spaces for writing. Chuck
Woodard and Kent Meyers had faith in my writing long
before I did. My early readers Jeanne Chaussee, Bong Kim,
Harriet Swedlund, Ginny Hatch, Ruby Wilson, Phyllis Cole-
Dai, Ruth Harper, Kathleen Donovan, and Sara Woster read
my early drafts. Patrick Thomas and Ben Barnhart guided
me toward the book this was meant to be. My siblings
Jeanne, Terry, Jim, and Kevin respected my version of the
story. Darla Biel, Joy Zarzana, Amber Jensen and Christine
Stewart never let me settle. Dan Lehman believed in this
book and patiently answered my questions. Larry Smith
took a leap of faith in publishing a first-time author. I am
grateful to all of you. My love to Maura, for becoming the
woman I imagined in the mirror, and to Ken, for always
being there.

REPRINT PERMISSIONS

Variations of chapters five, fifteen, and eight were
previously published as "Standing Naked in a Pool of her
Clothing," River Teeth, 2011, and Taking the Plunge, Passager
Magazine, 2009; "Honoring Ancestors," Notre Dame
Magazine, 2009, and "Woven in the Land," Platte Valley
Review, 2009.

Author's Note

In writing memoir, the writer must recreate events that have already happened, and because memory is a landscape of gaps and shadows, details are often unintentionally altered in the recreated story. I did intentionally compress the timeline and events in this book to facilitate ease in reading. Some names were changed to protect privacy. In writing about Korea, I relied on the journal in which I recorded conversations with Koreans, images from the places we visited, and my reflections on those experiences. To validate my notes as best possible, I consulted several books especially *Moon's Handbook on South Korea*, Robert Nilsen. Because of the many variant spellings in the Korean and Lakota words, I relied on *Moon's Handbook*, and the Akta Lakota Museum and Cultural Center in Chamberlain, South Dakota, for consistency in spelling and vocabulary.

PREFACE

The summer I was six I dug a hole to China. Inspired by a story my father liked to tell, I scratched at the packed dirt behind the tool shed on our central South Dakota farm with a tablespoon I had swiped from my mother's kitchen drawer. This was only a minor crime. She had tablespoons to spare; they were packed in fifty-pound sacks of Gold Medal Flour, and in her baking days, my mother bought a lot of flour.

My father would draw an imaginary globe in the air with his index finger, point to a spot at the top of the invisible sphere, and say, "Now, here is South Dakota." Never one to let science and reason deter him from a good story, he would trace a half-moon around the circle. With the other hand, he would draw a line down through the middle of the circle and say, "And here is China. Do you see how much farther the journey to China would be if you traveled around the earth instead of going directly through the center?"

All that summer, I worked on the hole, digging in the hard-packed sod with my tablespoon. When I began the excavation, I imagined a spot where the South Dakota ground met the China sky. There I would tumble through the hole into a land where men in yellow tunics and trousers ran barefoot over dirt roads as they pulled rickshaws, their faces shaded by wide, straw hats and single black braids bouncing against their backs. Inside the rickshaws, slender women in red silk dresses with mandarin collars and chopsticks in their hair hid their faces behind pleated fans painted with dragons and lotus flowers. For some reason, I could never imagine the faces of the people, nor picture the road they traveled.

After a while, I realized that despite hours of digging, I hadn't even penetrated the topsoil, and so I abandoned the project. If science and reason did not deter my father from telling a good story, it did deter his daughter from pursuing a practical impossibility. However, I never forgot his story of a journey to the other side of the world.

*   *   *

Many years later, I did drop out of the sky and fall into Asia, but I landed in South Korea, not China, a country nothing like the Asia of my imagination. My rickshaw was a Hyundai conveyance van driven by a middle-aged man wearing khaki pants, a fleece vest, and a Nike baseball cap. The dirt road was replaced by six lanes of concrete through miles of apartment buildings. And the woman behind the fan was Western-educated and fashionable in Ralph Lauren jeans, Levi jacket, and high-heeled leather boots. After traveling six thousand miles, I had finally crossed the border into Asia, but I felt as if I had circled back and landed in America.

My mother died in July 2004. Despite my age, I felt orphaned and homesick. Our daughter, Maura, was settled into a career and marriage in Minneapolis. My husband, Ken, sold the menswear store that had consumed his time and energy for thirty years, and he paced the house, restless and bored, checking the clock as if he had somewhere to be. I was growing weary of crawling out of bed to teach early morning classes and of serving on committees that endlessly debated crises recycled from my early teaching days. I was beginning to imagine being retired.

One afternoon I had coffee with the Director of International Studies at South Dakota State University. "You and Ken should go to Korea on the exchange program with Chungnam National University," she said. "It's a wonderful experience."

I thought about it on the drive home. I had often dreamed of living in a foreign country, the way my sister Jeanne had. But Korea didn't interest me. I knew nothing about the country except as the place America lost its first war or at least came home with no clear victory.

Still, I mentioned the exchange to Ken at supper that night. "I don't think I want to live in Korea."

He put down his fork, looked at me for a moment, and shrugged. "How will we know if we don't try it?"

We called our daughter, Maura, who had lived in England for over a year and traveled often. She slept with a desert tribe and rode a camel in Egypt, stood at the Wailing Wall in Jerusalem, ate bread and cheese in the shadow of the Eiffel Tower, and wandered the cobblestone streets of Prague.

"Of course you're going to do this," she said. "How often can you live in Asia?"

We hung up the phone and looked at each other. One of us said, although I'm not sure who, "Ok, let's do it." It was our most impulsive decision in nearly forty years of marriage.

PROLOGUE

In my dream, Ken and I drive down the dirt road that leads to my childhood farm pulled by a sliver of light shining through the dark. Suddenly, skeletal figures rise from the ditches, slide through the grain bin, and emerge from a silage pile. They come toward me, pale, shadowy, glowing figures who circle the car and chant: "Go back where you came from; you don't belong here. Go back. Go back."

I'm terrified, but fear compels me to drive on. I turn the corner, park under the rotting post with the shattered light bulb and rusty basketball hoop, and walk past the cistern with its smell of damp sand. The figures form a tunnel. As I walk through, they are so close I can see their eyes sunk into the hollows carved by the bones of their cheeks. They exhale puffs of dust and chant, "Go back. Go back."

The back porch where I once lay in my sick bed opens like a fan. The door to the left leads to the kitchen where apple pies cool on the kitchen counter and the fragrance of cinnamon perfumes the room. To the right is my bedroom where wallpaper with pink roses and trellises peels away from the plasterboard. The orange crate I painted yellow and used as a night stand sits in the middle of the room. In one corner, a plastic palomino lies on its side, legs splayed.

In a sunny corner of the living room, my father sits in his chair, a book in his hand. Our black lab, Nipper, rests his head on his knee, and my father runs his fingers through the dog's coarse hair as he reads. In the opposite corner is the upright piano where my mother should be sitting, but is not. Still ragtime and honky-tonk and the sound of children laughing rises.

I open the door and walk into the room. As I thread my way through a tangle of bones, cavities, and raggedy teeth, I hear. "Go away. She doesn't want you here."

A woman sits in a chair upholstered in brown-and-orange flowers. She is short and plump, with salt-and-pepper hair and pillowed breasts. She is my mother, and yet she is not my mother. She stares at me, her hazel eyes narrowed, her mouth corkscrewed as if trying to remember me.

"Please don't make me leave." I begin to weep. "I've traveled such a long way to come back here."

The woman's eyes fasten me to the floor. Then a glint of recognition, and a curve forms on her lips. She pushes herself out of the chair and walks toward me smiling, her arms open. I melt into the soft shape of my mother's love.

She traces spirals on my back. "It's ok," she whispers and then pulls me so close I can feel her heart beating in rhythm to mine and her apple-and-cinnamon breath warm against my cheek. "You're home now."

CHAPTER ONE

"What's so great about the truth?" my mother often asked. It wasn't a rhetorical question.

My mother's Irish parents burrowed their house beneath a grassy hill overlooking the prairie west of the Missouri River in South Dakota. They may have felt vulnerable in the wide, undulating grasslands of the Great Plains, so they pulled house and family inward as turtles retreat into shells. Or perhaps they feared being exposed. A clannish people by nature, their suspicion of outsiders was infused in their blood by memories of a repressive homeland. My father was the outsider who spoke the truth that lurked in the dark corners of their house.

My mother seldom spoke of the day her oldest brother fell ill and the family gathered around him. So I am left to recreate how the events unfolded. I imagine my grandparents, aunts, and uncles in the living room, the windows closed against the dust and heat of summer. The oldest son lies on his parents' bed, his face to the wall, the curtains drawn. My mother, a young woman, perches on a piano stool, her slender fingers lying still on her lap. The silence makes her anxious, and she longs to feel the comfort of piano keys under her fingertips. But this is no day for music.

There are whispered words Mother cannot hear. She looks at my grandmother, her eyebrows scrunched with worry. "It's nothing to be concerned about," my grandmother says. "Your brother has a migraine. Let's pray to the Blessed Mother to ease his pain."

The family kneels in a circle, their fingers moving over the rosary beads. "Hail Mary, full of Grace, the Lord is with thee." Surely my father knelt with them. But what was his prayer? For the right words, the right moment to tell his young wife the truth?

On the drive home, my father says, "You are old enough to know that your brother isn't sick; he's drunk." I see Mother's eyes flash and her jaw tighten. She walks into the one-room house, tucks the baby—my oldest brother—into

13

his spindled crib, and looks out the window at the star-stitched coverlet of night. "I was furious," she later told me. "I couldn't believe what he was saying. I just knew my brother didn't drink."

When I imagine that day, I see Mother turn away from the window. She accuses my father of lying and retreats into silence for days.

My mother learned early that truth could be spun like taffy into sweet evasions where hangovers are headaches and trips to the doctor merry outings.

"Hop in the car, kids. We're going for a ride." Mother smiled as she settled behind the steering wheel and tucked her handbag next to her hip. I jostled with my older siblings, the youngest sister looking for her place in the back seat. "Where are we going?"

"To town for ice cream."

As we drove over the bumpy road, I imagined the clinking of dimes on the bottom of her purse, the feel of silver slipping between my fingers as I handed the coins to the woman who would scoop ice cream out of a cardboard bin and layer it in a wafer cone.

But we stopped first at the clinic on Main Street where a nurse poked needles in our thin arms. Then Mother drove us to the ice cream parlor. We wore cotton balls taped over puncture wounds, and the smell of rubbing alcohol overpowered the aroma of cream and sugar. On the drive home, I fretted about the fib my mother told. The nuns said that fibs were venial sins that made God sad. What was so scary about truth that Mother would risk that? But when I looked at her face in the rear-view mirror, her eyes were clear. My worries melted with the taste of chocolate dripping from my fingers.

One day I would ask her, "Why didn't you tell us that we were getting vaccinations?"

She looked sheepish and annoyed at the question. "I only told a small fib. I wanted to protect you so you weren't afraid of getting a shot. Besides, what's so great about the truth?"

But evasions are sticky as taffy. In later years I couldn't ask why the doctors could not explain my father's rapid weight loss; why my mother sometimes lay in a dark room, an arm flung over her eyes; why she often seemed disappointed in me. I feared the truth as much as she did.

*   *   *

I sit in my sunroom in Brookings, South Dakota, tracing the pattern of vines and flowers inlaid in a box of shiny wood. On the lid, two fierce-eyed cranes made from bits of mollusk shells curve their wings around a lotus blossom as if to protect it from rough winds or insistent waves. Their wings glitter in the sunlight.

"This is a *najeon chilgi,* a lacquer jewelry box," I remember Dr. Han saying.

Dr. Han, a man with spiky hair and lively eyes who taught economics at Chungnam National University, was our good friend during my time as visiting professor there. He stopped by our apartment the week we arrived with a small package. Gift giving in Korean culture requires the Confucian propriety of ceremony, so he bowed before extending the package toward me with both hands. "It's only a small thing," he said. To suggest the gift is unworthy of the receiver's status demonstrates the virtue of humility.

The gift was wrapped in *hanji,* delicate, handcrafted paper made from a mulberry tree and speckled with bits of bark. I unfolded the paper carefully. I wanted to take it home, perhaps frame it and hang it above my desk. Or use it to wrap a gift for someone special. Inside the wrapping paper was a black box covered with bits of sea shells.

"Those shells are nacre from abalone and conch shells found on the beaches of Jeju-do, an island off the southern tip of the peninsula," he said.

"What is the translation of nacre?"

"You would call it mother of pearl. Nacre is the layer that mollusks build around themselves to protect their soft parts."

In the summer of 1952, when I was seven years old, I lay in a children's ward in a hospital in Mitchell, South Dakota. The room smelled of antiseptic and feverish dreams. Through the silence, I could hear whimpering and the rustling of sheets as children tossed in their sleep. Through the bars of my hospital bed, I could see their faces, translucent in the moon's light. But there was no comfort in their company. They were simply objects, as I was. We lay in the moonlight like sea shells washed up on the shore.

Had I asked my mother why she left me alone in this dark hospital ward, she would have spoken of the harvest and my father in the fields, of older siblings and a baby brother at home, of her tears when the nuns told her visiting hours were over and sent her back to the farm miles away.

But no words could ease my feelings of being abandoned or dispel my fears that I was being punished for something, though I didn't know what.

Maybe she had seen me when I did the naughtiest thing I could imagine. Was my mother peeking out the window in disappointment as I dropped my panties and urinated just so I could watch the yellow stream snake through the cracked dirt? Was my mother worn out by nursing me through bouts of fever and painful limbs, the effects of rheumatic fever when I was three? Had she finally left me in the care of the nuns while she went home to be with children who weren't so demanding?

A white figure glided into the room, woolen clouds floating around her, the faint scent of bleach in the air. "How are you feeling?"

"Fine," I said, even though loneliness pressed against my bones and I longed to feel my mother's freckled arms curved around me as she rocked me to sleep.

A hand touched my cheek. "You can tell me the truth."

If I admitted to the nun that I felt abandoned, she might tell my mother, and maybe the next night, Mother would insist on sleeping in a chair next to my crib as she had those many nights in that other hospital. But if I confessed to feeling neglected by my mother, who prided herself on being a good mother, she would be devastated. If I had to choose between seeing her eyes cloud over at my betrayal or spending more lonely nights in the hospital, I would choose to lie.

"I'm fine," I said. I turned away from the nun, coiled into the folds of my blanket, and buried my face in the pillow.

"Making a lacquer box is a painstaking process," Dr. Han said. He mimicked the work with his hands as he talked—gluing the pieces of wood together, covering the box in hemp, brushing layers of lacquer over the surface, and feathering bits of shell into the varnish.

Remembering Dr. Han's instructions, "Hold the box in the sunlight and watch what happens when you tilt it back and forth," I walk to the window of our sunroom. When I tilt the box one way, the colors of the shells are an impressionistic painting shimmering over the yellow walls. At a different angle, deer, cranes, and chrysanthemums are distinct in the iridescent shells. Often memory is blurry as well. But sometimes when the angle of the light is just right, a clear scene emerges.

*　　　*　　　*

I sat cross-legged on the kitchen floor cutting paper dolls from the Montgomery Ward's catalog. The room was sunny, and it might have smelled of coffee, certainly of apple pies baking. I imagine steam roiling from a pot on the range and drifting across the ceiling. Surely, a canary warbled in its cage, and chicken sizzled in a frying pan. The phone rang. My mother turned off the gas burner and scurried to answer it. She gasped. I looked up to see her lips pressed together and her eyes wide. She held the phone to her ear. Her head drooped so low her chin touched the ruffle on her apron. She must have said something that told me my grandmother had died, but I don't remember the words.

The blueprints of our lives are etched in moments like these.

My mother was a young woman when her mother died. I think time may have stopped for her that day, so she would always see my grandmother as a perfect mother—present and devoted to her children. "I wanted to be just like my mother," she often said. But did she ever imagine my grandmother when she had been a teacher in the days before her marriage? Did she ever wonder if her mother had dreams that did not include husband and children? Dreams of a life beyond the grasslands?

I am a mirror image of my mother—stocky and buxom, irreverent and sardonic, quick to laugh but not to weep. She was a wonderful mother for a young girl. She was never critical of my clothes or my grades. She often said she was proud of me. She was the most popular of all the mothers because she never griped if my friends dragged mud into the house or left a mess in the kitchen when we made fudge. She was funny but unpredictable—mostly a nervous and hovering mother but now and then detached and distracted, leaving me confused about how mothers should act. But I never doubted or disagreed with her when she said, "Children must always come first." What I heard was women belong in the home. I thought I would be a mother just like her.

When I went to graduate school, I read feminist authors for the first time—Adrienne Rich, Kate Chopin, Charlotte Perkins Gilman, Virginia Woolf. At the same time, I was learning more about the feminist movement. Bella Abzug, flamboyant as her hats, stood behind a bank of microphones arguing for equality at the workplace and reproductive rights. Betty Friedan was a founder of the National Organization for Women and wrote *The Feminine*

Mystique. Gloria Steinem helped launch *Ms. Magazine.* I began to question my old assumptions. I formed opinions that differed from Mother's.

"Women should be priests," I said. I didn't listen to her murmuring about altering centuries of tradition.

"We need more women in public office and running corporations," I argued. I ignored her, "But who will care for the children?"

I was so caught up in redefining myself as a woman that I didn't see how her shoulders tightened when I said such things. Years later when I cleaned out her house, I discovered a poem my grandmother wrote when my mother graduated from high school. She added the inscription, "If you never cause anyone more grief than you have me, your life will be well spent. From Your Mother, the one who knows you best." How often had my mother studied me with narrowed eyes as if she didn't recognize her own daughter?

One day she said, "I never disagreed with my mother. I always tried to please her." Mother spoke so softly I didn't hear the undertone of anger.

There was in my mother a thin line between fear and anger.

On August 19, 1968, the year I became both a college graduate and a new bride, Ken and I made a frantic trip to Chamberlain, South Dakota. My brother Jim had called to say, "You need to come home. Dad is dying." We pulled up to my parents' house at the same time as my mother and siblings. "Oh, you're too late," she said. "I'm sorry, but your dad died an hour ago."

Although I knew my father's illness was terminal, I wasn't prepared for how quickly it progressed. I thought we would have months, perhaps a year, to say goodbye. But he went about the work of dying with the same speed and efficiency that he worked the fields. He died nine weeks to the day after he was diagnosed.

Mother came toward me carrying a plastic bag that contained my father's glasses, wallet, and wrist watch. But suddenly she turned, marched into the garage, and tossed the bag in a garbage can. Then she went into the house to make coffee. I stood in the dark for several minutes. I could find no words to explain such raw emotion from my normally stoic mother. Later, my brother Terry retrieved the sack and set it on Mother's dresser.

I couldn't sleep that night, so I slipped out of the covers and went to my mother's room where she and my sister lay on the bed, their backs propped against the pillows. I curled up at their feet, listening to Mother tell stories about my father. "I'll never forget the surprise on his face when he bit into fried fish and got a mouthful of scales. I didn't know I was supposed to scale fish.

"Or the time he jumped into the cattle tank because he thought your brother Jim was thrashing in the water. I can still see him standing covered in moss when the dog, not Jim, crawled out of the tank and trotted across the feedlot. That was so funny."

We laughed and cried until the pink and gold hues of daybreak fanned over the river bluffs. Then Mother got out of bed and went to the kitchen to make coffee for the stream of visitors who would come that day.

The morning of the funeral, she stood by the hearse as the pallbearers lifted my father's casket to their shoulders. Her face was ashen in the August sun, and her shoulders inverted like a wounded bird's. When she turned to follow the casket, her knees seemed to buckle and her hands flew up as if to grab something. She caught herself, straightened her shoulders, and led her dazed children across the buffalo grass to bury their father.

As we walked back to the car, I saw something different in her eyes, a hard edge I'd never seen before. She was fifty years old, widowed, and a single mother of a teenage boy. She had never balanced the checkbook, never filled a car with gasoline or changed filters on a furnace, and she knew nothing about managing the farm she now owned. Mother had only been angry at us when we wandered too close to the power takeoff or dangled from the high crosspieces of the windmill. Widowed so young, she must have been terrified by what lay ahead for her. Fear turned to anger at my father for dying, at the doctor who treated his stomach pains for months as stress-related ulcers, at God perhaps, and even at that small sack that held my father's possessions.

"Lacquer boxes were once used to hold wooden *malas* or *sutras*, the Mahayana texts something like your Christian Bible," Dr. Han told me. "But today women keep jewelry and secret treasures like love letters in their *najeon chilgi*."

My lacquer box holds a secret treasure—a mirror tucked inside the lid and in the glass my mother's face looking back at me. I have already seen this inversion of our faces in a grainy photo—my pug nose, heavy-lidded eyes, and thick bangs sweeping across a wide forehead, looking back at my mother from a large mirror leaning against the handlebars of a tricycle. She is a small girl in a dress with a smocked bodice and a wide collar trimmed in rickrack. Her bare feet rest against the trike's pedals, and I can almost feel the metal pressing into her flesh. She cocks her head and studies my face in the mirror as if the camera had captured the child looking at the woman her daughter will become, while the adult woman considers the small girl her mother once was.

When I was twenty-eight, I harbored a terrible secret. I was pregnant, but I didn't think I wanted to be a mother. I was happy with my life. My marriage was good, and my career as an English professor at South Dakota State University was rewarding. I didn't know how to make room for anything more. When I saw my nieces and nephews tugging at their mothers' legs or crawling like a litter of kittens over their grandmother's lap, I didn't smile as I thought of the day children would clamor over me. Rather, I felt those needy hands would pull me apart, one piece at a time until I was only a resentful shell.

I smiled when people congratulated me and laughed at the jokes about my expanding belly. I nodded, although I didn't understand, when my sister said, "Now your life will be complete." At night as I lay awake listening to Ken's breathing, I sometimes lifted my pajama top and spread my fingers over my belly feeling for the fine bones. In the moonlight, my taut skin was luminous as pearls. I tried to imagine the tiny being curled beneath the protective layers of my womb. Sometimes a foot pressed against me like the weight of my pretense.

The doctor told me that the baby would absorb whatever sustenance it needed from me as it developed. But what would be left of me, I wondered, once the baby had taken all that it needed? What strain would a child put on my marriage? On my career? Did other women feel this way or would they be shocked by my confession? I longed to ask Mother if she ever feared being sucked dry by motherhood. But I remembered how often she said, her eyes shining, "All I ever wanted was to be full of babies." How could I admit to her that I was an empty shell of a woman?

The first time I held Maura, she looked at me with confident eyes as if she never doubted my love for her. I held her to my breasts, rested my cheek against her downy hair, and breathed in the smell of her as we rocked in the glow of the nightlight. I felt a love I didn't know was possible and relief that I was meant for the role of mother. Yet I knew that being a mother still wasn't enough for me.

I never dreamed she'd give up on her children. I heard my mother's voice in my head as I dropped Maura off at day care and walked to the university, my heels clicking on pavement.

I first heard Mother say these words when I was a little girl and a neighbor lady walked by our house on her way to work, a little peacock of a woman whom I always imagine wearing a royal-blue pencil skirt, frilly blouse, and clunky red jewelry. Her heels clicked as she strutted down the sidewalk on the way to the city hall where she was a secretary. She was the only mother I knew at the time who worked outside the home. She was a woman I never intended to become.

Years later, I, too, was a working mother. I relished the creativity and curiosity of my colleagues and the energy of my students as they navigated their college careers. My schedule was often overloaded with Maura's school activities and homework clashing with committee meetings and grading papers. But I couldn't imagine staying home. Still, the words "I never dreamed she'd give up on her children" were folded into my happiness.

Then I read Kate Chopin's novel *The Awakening,* the story of Edna Pontellier, a New Orleans woman who resists social conventions imposed on women in the late nineteenth century. At one point in the novel, Edna says, "I would give up my life for my children. But I wouldn't give up myself."

I read the words again, and then again. Something clicked. Those words explained what I felt and gave me permission to feel that way. I would die for Maura, but I could not lose myself in her. I felt as if a burden I didn't know I carried had been lifted from me.

I'm still not sure why I read that passage to Mother. Being a literature teacher, I may have thought we were on safe ground discussing a fictional character who could speak a truth I was afraid to tell. More likely, I thought I had found a clever way to win the silent argument between us. When I finished reading, she pressed her tongue against her teeth and said nothing.

21

"I want to help you understand," I said. "I'm a happier mother because I have kept a part of myself by working." She stared at the floor.

I kept pressing my point, a little girl seeking her mother's approval. "Mother, you devoted your life to your children, and I appreciate that. You were a wonderful mother."

Still, she said nothing. The conversation was cheap fireworks that didn't explode but fizzled into silence. I was so desperate to justify my choices to her, or perhaps to myself, I forgot how easily her fears merged into anger. I didn't consider that she may have feared feminists like her daughter would dismantle the things she valued the way I dismantled the house she inhabited for forty years—sorting through pots and pans, cookbooks, photo albums, clothes, china teacups and knickknacks, rosaries, and sheet music. I packed some in boxes, discarded others. When I was done, a threadbare carpet and empty cupboards were all that remained.

"Why can't you understand? I'm trying to be truthful. I'm not like you. I need to be more."

Mother froze. My hand flew over my mouth as if to trap the words. I could smell the chalk on my fingers left from teaching that day. It mingled with the sour smell of regret. Across the street, college girls sang to a boom box blasting from their rented duplex. *Ba boom, ba boom, ba boom.* But the silence in my house was louder and more powerful.

Mother stared at the floor, her shoulders slumped. Finally she said, "I can't believe a daughter of mine would say that."

I had at last spoken my truth, but the words were clumsy and hurtful. I meant to say I wanted to be like her and yet different as well. But there was no way to take back my words. They hung between us like clothes on a line in winter—frigid and unbending.

Mother was right to believe that there was nothing special about the truth. I began to build a shell around me, layers of silence upon layers of unspoken truths so that I would never again hurt my mother like that. Truthfully, though, I meant to protect myself from her anger.

Dr. Han said that lacquer used in making *najeon chilgi* comes from lacquer trees found in the hills of the Kangwan Province. Small incisions are made in the bark, and buckets hang from the trunk to catch the sap that becomes the varnish. I run my fingers over my lacquer box. The shells under the layers of varnish are smooth beneath my fingertips.

"It is a varnish so strong that it will hold the bits of shells forever," Dr. Han said. "The beauty of lacquer boxes is their delicate yet permanent nature, and so Koreans see them as a symbol of enduring love."

The call came on a warm September evening just as dusk was falling. My brother Kevin said, "Mother had a heart attack and they're airlifting her to the hospital. It doesn't look good." As I drove to the hospital, the grasses on the hills along the interstate were layers of light and shadow in the moonlight. They mirrored the overlap of love, regret, and fear I felt.

Mother underwent triple bypass and valve replacement. Within a week after surgery, pus oozed from the incision running down her chest and she was prepped once again for surgery. The doctor came into the waiting room where my brothers and I paced. "We will scrape out the staph infection in her chest cavity. The plan is to leave the incision open so we treat the infection with medicated gauze. Her chances of survival are about ten percent."

For five days, I sat in a corner of the intensive care unit nauseated by the faint odor of illness layered beneath the smell of Lysol. The machines whirred and luminous numbers blinked on a computer screen. The medical team was a blur of green draped over my mother, their words a foreign language I would never master. One day I saw hands immersed in my mother's open chest cavity as the nurse packed medicated gauze into the wound. I wanted to wrap my arms around my fragile mother, to shield her from this violation. At the same time, I was in awe of that moment when another woman touched my mother's heart.

Despite the bleak chances of Mother surviving the infection, she lived another five years. I took her out to lunch often during those last days. We laughed at stories about her childhood that I never heard before. "One time I peeked through the crack in the barn wood and thought I saw a pig hanging from the rafter. But it was your grandpa standing in a tub of water taking a bath. I'd never seen a naked person before." She laughed, but her cheeks flushed at the memory. I saw ovals of pink buttocks on a grandpa I never knew.

"We went to dances every Saturday night. My brothers were great dancers and so much fun." She didn't mention the fights behind the dance hall. She didn't talk about the cuts and bruises on her brother's faces, the hangovers the next morning. I didn't worry about revisions of the truth in the stories she told. What did truth matter now?

After lunch, we shopped at Younker's cosmetics department where a woman with flawless makeup and kind eyes took Mother's elbow and eased her onto a stool. "So what will we try today, Marie?"

The salesclerk uncoiled a tube of lipstick and handed it to my mother. I stood behind Mother as she dabbed lipstick on her lips. There is something intimate about watching a woman put on makeup, something unguarded in her eyes as she studies her reflection. Our faces in the looking glass, just inches apart, were those I see whenever I open my lacquer box. Perhaps this was the moment when we could be honest with one another, and I could ask the questions that haunted me. Had life turned out the way she had imagined as a young woman? Was I the daughter she had dreamed of? But I didn't ask. I told myself she didn't have the strength for such questions. In truth, silence was too engrained in me.

Mother picked up a cut-glass atomizer from the shelf, pumped the rubber bulb, and sprayed perfume in the hollows of her neck. Then she rubbed lotion over her gnarled hands, slowly and thoughtfully, her eyes closed. I tried to memorize her face in the mirror, her square jaw, the depressions in her temples, her deep-set eyes. But I knew her image would fade over time, leaving only my face in the mirror to remember her by. She wrapped her fingers around my arm and leaned against me as she slid off the stool. I took her back to her apartment.

On the drive home, the fragrance of gardenias lingered in the car.

CHAPTER TWO

Oh, son of a biscuit, Mother gripes from her distant grave. *There's a bird flu epidemic right now, and you'll never find a doctor in this god-forsaken country.*

I hear her voice as I stagger down the jetway at Seoul's Incheon Airport. I am nauseated from the lack of sleep and the smell of diesel fuel and stale morning breath of the passengers around me. I bump into a woman wearing white gloves and a surgical mask. She backs away, folds her hands over her middle, and bows. When I see her mask, I feel my stomach knot with the foreboding instilled in children of nervous mothers. How does bird flu spread? Droplets in the air? Contact?

We had been told that only a handful of bird flu cases had been reported in Korea, which Koreans attribute to eating *kimchi,* the fermented cabbage that is the quint-essential Korean dish. Now I fear those reports are wrong, and my mother's predictions will at last come true. I will die in a pandemic.

Mother kept a mental rolodex of disasters—drowning in stock ponds, tetanus from rusty nails, rattlesnake bites, failed brakes on mountain roads, and runaway horses. The last she offered on principle; we didn't own a horse. When I began to travel more frequently for work and pleasure, she mailed articles to me with ominous headlines:

"Outbreaks of Foot-and-Mouth in British Isles."

"Invasion of Legionnaires' Disease in New York."

I didn't read the clippings, but I didn't discard them either. I tossed them in a mushroom cookie jar she made in ceramics class. (Poisonous mushrooms were also on her list.) I tucked the jar behind canisters of flour and sugar. The elf sitting on the lid peeked at me through the Tupperware. Maybe I kept the clippings because I worried if I threw them away I would die of foot-and-mouth or Legionnaires' disease. My certainty of retribution for ignoring my mother's advice began when I was six or seven and I, on a dare, shoplifted a Pez dispenser from the Five and Dime

25

Store. That night I lay in bed hearing the clanging of doors on jail cells. I saw my mother staring at me through the bars. "What did I tell you about stealing?" Sometimes when I passed by the jar, I imagined the smell of damp earth and saw death caps and destroying angels sprouting in moldy newsprint.

I hear her voice again. *For Pete's sake, what are you thinking traipsing off to some dang country on the other side of the world?*

Had I traipsed to Korea to quiet my mother's voice? To escape the memories that often haunt me? If so, Korea is no place to run from your past, for in Korea the line between the living and the dead is malleable and the spirits of the ancestors inhabit the living world for four generations before departing to the next one. So, too, the spirit of my mother—that reluctant traveler—found the gumption to travel six thousand miles so she could insert herself in my days here.

Ahead of me, Ken weaves easily through the airport crowd, unaware of the dangers that I am now certain await us. I stumble behind him, dragging my overnight case, my backpack knocking into other travelers. Why had I agreed to this exchange with Chungnam National University? Had I put us both in danger by moving here? At the baggage carousel, I grab his arm and whisper, "Ken, look at all the masks. What if there's an epidemic? Do you think we should go home?"

He shrugs. "I'm sure it's nothing to worry about. Do you see your duffle bag?"

I am annoyed and envious at how calm he remains in the face of catastrophe, the way Mother must have felt the few times I ignored her warnings. *I know things but nobody wants to listen to me.* (Those words often popped out of my mouth when I was raising a teenage daughter.) We collect our bags and walk to passport control. While the officer inspects our documents, we spot Ms. Lim, our CNU liaison, pacing the rope barrier and waving to us. She runs up to us, bows, and says, "Hello, welcome to Korea. I will be the one to help you during your time here."

She signals to a middle-aged man and woman who stand at the revolving door at the entrance—her mother and the driver of the conveyance van. They grab our luggage and muscle their way through taxis idling at the curbside. We trail behind them guided by taillights glowing in the dark. We drive out of Incheon Airport past miles of high-rise apartments, their windows light and dark like electronic chess boards. I lean my cheek against the van's window, staring at the lights. Will we be fate's pawn in days to come?

After twenty-seven hours of travel, we finally arrive at our new home, a three-hundred-square-foot apartment on the seventh floor of a women's dormitory. Ken opens the window to let the winter air freshen the room. I walk barefoot over the warm *ondol* floor—Korean homes are heated by a system of pipes beneath the floor—exploring the apartment. The kitchen is a half wall of cupboards with a two-burner hot plate on the counter, a refrigerator, and a low Korean table with no chairs or floor cushions. I open one cabinet door—nothing. Another door—empty. In the other room are twin beds, two desks, and two empty wardrobes. The bathroom, no bigger than a packing crate, is empty as well, except for a dingy towel hanging on a rack and a bar of soap pooling in scum.

"Ken, how are we going to get by with so little?"

I'm not encouraged by his optimism. "Hey, we'll figure something out. There are stores in Korea. We can buy things."

I feel the familiar tension of my childhood, the pull of a mother who wrapped her children in a cocoon of caution against the push of a father who urged us to peel away the layers of fear so we might experience the world. For most of my life, even now after their deaths, I have danced their waltz of advance and retreat.

In many ways I share my father's wanderlust, which I consider a gift and Mother considered a character flaw. If the rains made the fields too muddy to plow or the calves were born and waiting to wean, he crammed his five children, our dog, and my mother into our 1956, nine-passenger Pontiac station wagon—white with turquoise stripes—pulled out of the farmyard, and barreled down our dirt lane. When we turned onto the gravel road, he gripped the steering wheel with his broad hands and grappled with the car as it fishtailed over ridges of loose stones, raising smoke signals of dust that warned other cars of our speedy approach. Once he turned onto the oiled surface of Highway 16, he relaxed his grip on the wheel and sang "See them tumbling down. . . . pledging their love to the ground."

Sometimes I am like that—open to possibilities—and eager to take risks like the summer Ken and I drove a rental car around Ireland, lost on back roads and city streets. We were like kids backpacking Europe with no plans except to find pubs that offered pints of Smithwicks and chats with the locals, no obligations besides finding a country bed and breakfast with a hostess who would serve us brown bread and whiskey-laced porridge. My stomach didn't knot once on that trip; being lost was an adventure I relished. But other times, like now, for reasons I can't explain, I am my mother pacing a dark, unfamiliar room cataloging how little we possess for the next six months—our clothes, a few books, a laptop, and the water bottle I carried with me from the Minneapolis airport.

Ken, born late in his parent's marriage, was also raised by an anxious mother. When she spotted a red mark on his skin, she mixed a poultice of bread and milk and caked the spot with the paste. She made him choke down castor oil and, when he was sick, milk toast. But despite her hovering, he never lost the spirit of a boy looking for adventure. Over the years, I have followed him over railroad tracks in deep grass, down ravines to wade in streams, and up mountain trails. Now he sleeps across the room, his breathing soft and regular. The moonlight falls over his thick lashes and casts shadows on his cheekbones. His hands are open on the coverlet.

Finally, too exhausted to worry any more, I crawl under the cover and fall asleep. Moments later, gongs blast me awake, and I hear a male voice speaking in a foreign tongue, an ominous sound in my jet-lagged haze. I leap out of bed. There's a fire. Where's the fire escape?

The next morning Steve, who teaches in the Foreign Language Institute, will tell us that the gongs alert students to announcements. "That's the residential hall manager. He's telling the students about events coming up and reminding them about dorm rules."

"But there are no students right now," I say.

He laughs. "Not only that, but he's speaking Korean in an English-only dormitory. Welcome to Korea, where somehow there is clarity in its contradictions. You're going to be changed by living here."

I almost ask what kind of change, but I don't. I'm not certain I want the answer. That afternoon Steve will come to our apartment and help Ken disconnect the intercom.

But right now I panic. "Ken, what do those gongs mean?"

He lifts his head. "Huh?"

"What is he saying? Do something."

He does. He rolls over and goes back to sleep.

I stumble into the kitchen, brace the door open with a shoe, and creep down the hallway. The voice follows me as I wander through empty apartments. There is a hint of something vinegary and fishy in the rooms. It was one of the many cooking odors I detected at a truck stop earlier that night. Strange, pungent smells nothing like those that remind me of other countries we had visited—cream and butter in France, tomatoes and basil in Italy, pineapple and *sofrito* in Jamaica. The truck stop smelled of sea, soil, and dried blood, aromas I later learn are *bbundaegi,* boiled silkworm, and *soondeh,* blood sausage, and *kimchi.*

Finally the voice stops. I trudge back to our apartment, sit on the bed, lean against the wall, and count the months until we fly home. The concrete is cold against my back. I shiver and pull my legs to my chest, a pose I remember seeing in a photo of my mother on the front stoop of her family's house. She wears a straw hat and overalls and a blouse printed in flowers. She clasps her hands around her knees and curls her shoulders inward. Sunflowers growing by the foundation tower over her tiny frame. She looks childlike and vulnerable.

I feel vulnerable and unprepared for the months to come. I long for the emergency kit Mother stowed beneath her feet on our road trips—a thermometer and Vicks Vapor Rub, bottles of Pepto-Bismol and castor oil, Band-Aids and mercurochrome. If one of us looked flushed, she reached into the bag, grabbed an aspirin, and stuck it in our mouths, leaving the sour taste of granules crumbling beneath dry tongues.

As I fall asleep that night I hear my mother's voice from years ago. *And just where will you be finding a doctor in this god-forsaken country,* she asks my father as we drive through the salt flats of Utah, the spiraling highways of the Big Horn Mountains, and the milky-way lit prairies of Canada.

Behind our apartment is a network of trails running up the side of a mountain, and we follow the path to a spot that overlooks the city. Daejeon, the capital of the Chungcheongnam-do Province, begins in the narrow corridor of the mountains and spills out into the plains. The Charyeong Mountain range runs through city, and the Geum River switches directions here. Beyond the mountains are Gyeryeong-san National Park, Buddhist temples, and monasteries. Down the hill to the south is Yuseong, where natural hot springs feed spas that draw tourists to its hotels, casinos, restaurants, and brothels hidden in alleys.

The population of the province is nearly two million people, with more than a million and a half living in Daejeon. Like the rest of the country, the Daejeon area is seventy percent mountainous, and high-rise apartments painted white with black trim are stacked like dominoes for miles. Four hundred and seventy-two people inhabit a square mile of this city. In Lyman County where I grew up, two people inhabit a square mile of grassland. There will be many days when I feel energized by the crowds pushing and shoving on the sidewalks, by the smell of espresso from sun-filled coffee shops and roasted silkworms at a street market, by the wailing of sirens merging into disco from karaoke rooms. But other times, I will feel claustrophobic and desperate for a piece of land where sky and earth are seamless, a place so quiet I can hear only the wind whispering to the grass.

On those days I will hike to the top of this hill and turn in a circle until my internal compass points to Medicine Butte, a summit that rises twenty-seven-hundred feet above the grassland west of our farm. Paha Pejuta is a holy place for the Lakota people who hold sacred ceremonies on its flat top. It is a landmark that has guided me since I was a small girl sitting on my mother's lap and peering out the windshield looking for the butte's sandstone-colored sides to tell me I was close to home. If I close my eyes, the city buildings disappear and the noise of traffic fades until there is only sky, silence, and the feel of my mother's arms around me as we drive home. I begin to breathe again.

At the top of the hill is a *jeongmangdae*—a gazebo with ceiling and posts covered in vividly painted lotus blossoms, pomegranates, dragons, and cranes—symbols of wisdom, fertility, a long life, and peace. This traditional decorative pattern called *tanch'ong* is meant not only to decorate buildings, but to protect the wood and to cover its flaws. *Tanch'ong* is displayed throughout Korea on beams in temples and palaces, picnic shelters, and museums.

Ken says, "I'm going to take that path down the other side of the hill and see what's there. Wanna come?"

"No, I think I'll sit a bit on this bench." I don't tell him that I want some quiet time to reflect on the day before when I wandered the narrow streets of Gung Dong, the shopping district below the hill. The street was redolent with the smell of garbage, fish on beds of ice, and something spicy wafting from a nearby restaurant. Elderly Korean men and women scuttled over the sidewalks, sorting through yellow squash and sweet potatoes, eggplant and spinach, garlic and red chili peppers—earth-bound rainbows that fanned across the concrete. I stopped to admire the produce, wishing I had a well-stocked kitchen so I could prepare *bibimbap*, a dish made with *gochujan*—fiery red pepper paste—rice, grilled beef, and slivers of raw vegetables.

Across the street an old woman sat cross-legged on the sidewalk huddling, over a basket of squash, carrots, and cabbage. She wore baggy pants, a tattered sweater, and a scarf coiled around her neck. Her skin was leathered from working outdoors, except for a pale scalp beneath her thin, gray hair. Crowds pushed and shoved on the sidewalk near her as they rushed to catch a bus rumbling to a stop at the corner. She seemed out of time and place in this frenzied city, and I imagined a day when her hair was dark and thick, and she toiled in a rice field, her linen trousers a lotus flower blossoming in the muddy water. I stood in the middle of the crosswalk, staring at her while students swirled around me like currents around a sandbar.

The street vendor's eyes tugged at me. As I wove through the crowd toward her, I saw my mother clutching my sister's arm as she teetered between tables in a crowded restaurant and then collapsed into a chair. Mother ordered a sandwich she didn't touch and a cup of coffee that was soon cold and covered with a film of cream. I ordered a salad I didn't eat.

It was only a few weeks before my mother died, and we were having lunch because she insisted that we take her to Minerva's, her favorite restaurant. I babbled to distract myself from seeing my mother slumped in her chair, her breath coming in short spurts. "So," I said, "You won't be surprised to hear that Maura and Steve are going to Jamaica to celebrate their first anniversary."

I knotted the napkin in my damp hands, waiting, hoping, that she would complain as she always did about Maura traipsing around the world. "Humph, that girl is crazy. Can't she stay home?"

But she didn't seem to hear. I felt the tablecloth quivering against my thighs.

At the table next to us, a woman said to the waiter, "This isn't what I ordered." The waiter returned with a different plate of food. How simple to change an order in a restaurant. How difficult to exchange this painful moment for another one, perhaps a day when my mother sits at the piano, her fingers flying over the keys, her fleshy body bouncing on the stool as women dance in our living room; my mother chortling with my Irish aunties as they worked in the kitchen preparing Sunday dinners; Mother serving apple pie and lemonade to her weight loss club on a steamy night in July; Mother on Christmas Eve rolling dough into pillows she stuffed with stewed fruit.

The old street vendor pulled one hand out of a ragged sleeve and pointed to a bundle of *tang geun*. Beside her, my mother lifted a finger to brush away a strand of hair from her cheek and studied me with eyes that reflected frustration, pride, and love. I longed to stroke the old woman's hair and finger the red threads that zigzagged through her scarf. I longed to feel her fingers brushing my face. But instead, I picked out a bundle of carrots, placed a few *won* in her outstretched hand, and moved on.

The sun begins its descent behind the mountains and casts shadows over the trees and the rooftops. The colorful images on the beams darken. The streetlights flicker, and the rumble of rush-hour traffic dims. I leave the *jeongmangdae* and trek down the rocky path toward Ken, who waits at the bottom of the trail. In the dusk, I don't see a root pushing up from the dirt, and I stumble. I grab a tree branch to steady myself.

Oh, for God's sake, you're gonna fall down and break your dang fool neck.

"I know, Mother," I whisper. "I know."

I wrap my hand around the branch of one tree and then another. Clinging to one branch at a time, I make my cautious way through the fading light back down the hill to our apartment.

CHAPTER THREE

Slender fingers loop and twist a strand of red silk as fine as hair into spirals until it forms a heart-shaped knot, perhaps an inch or two across. Then the weaver works the strand backwards to its starting point.

I point to the knot and ask, "*Myeot?*" What is it?

The woman brings her fingers to her mouth and nibbles. "*Ddalgi. Ddalgi.*" Strawberry, the fruit of healing and new beginnings.

I am wandering through the crowds at The Super Lotte Department store, a warehouse-sized room that feels more like a street market than a retail store. Shoppers squeeze between tables stacked with small appliances, linens, clothing, pharmaceuticals, cleaning supplies, packaged groceries, and cooking utensils. Vendors shout to one another over the chatter of cash registers. The aroma of *mul naengmyeon*—cold buckwheat noodles in beef broth—mingles with the earthy smell of *bbundaegi*—boiled silkworms.

In the middle of the room is a kiosk with shelves of wooden statues, brass lanterns, ceremonial masks, lacquered boxes, and gilded statuettes of Buddha. A glass case displaying tasseled ornaments and racks of rainbow-colored threads catches my eye, as does the woman who stands behind the counter.

She wears a light-gray c*higori,* a loose blouse with pink lotus blossoms embroidered on the collar. The hem of her *hanbok chima* is trimmed with the same pattern. Silver hair sweeps away from her cheeks to expose a broad forehead. Her smile reveals a gap between her front teeth. Remembering that is rude for a Korean woman to show her teeth, she quickly covers her mouth with her hand. Her brown eyes are inquisitive. Perhaps she wonders how a Westerner discovered this out-of-the way market. As a shrewd business owner, she may be deciding how to bridge the language gap with a potential customer. As I approach her, she bows. "*Annyeong haseyo.*"

33

I bow as well. *"Annyeong haseyo."*

Around her neck hangs a chain of threads in rich plum tones that connects a cylindrical pink stone to rows of fringes. I point at her necklace, nod my head, and say *"Areumdaun,"* hoping that she understands I'm trying to say "beautiful."

She bows and says, *"Kamsahamnida."* She slips out of rubber flip flops, steps outside the kiosk, and puts on a pair of heels. She bows again so deeply that beneath her top I can see the rosettes of bones that connect her spine. Then she pulls a tray of tasseled ornaments out of the cabinet. I raise my eyebrows to ask, "What are these?"

The woman picks out a tasseled ornament with the yin-yang symbol embroidered in primary colors and attached to strings of knots in cobalt blue and sea green. Rummaging through a drawer, she finds a piece of scrap paper and a pencil, writes the word *maedeup,* underlines it, and then points to the handiwork in the display case.

I nod, *"Ye."* Yes.

Knot tying dates back to fifty-seven BC. There is a Korean saying that life begins and ends with a knot. While giving birth, women clenched knotted cords that hung over their beds. At their deaths, the mourners tied decorative knots to the corners of their flower-covered biers. For a time it was seen as folk art, the craft of peasants and farmers, and the practice was dying. In the 1960's, an artist named Jeon Yeon Su revived the art of Korean knotting. Today, Koreans consider the art form to be a bridge connecting the present to the past from fingertips to fingertips of women. It has flourished in the hands of this woman who weaves symbols of maternal love and desires into the knots and who now extends her business card. It reads Beauty of Korea, the name of her store.

I point to an ornament with a butterfly embroidered in lavender and rose threads and interwoven with filaments of gold. Hoping again that she understands my clumsy Korean, I say, *"Chom?"* Please may I pick this up? She nods. The craftsmanship is evident in the way that the front and back of the butterfly mirror one another and in the symmetry of the chrysanthemum's blossoms. I run my fingers over the threads. They bring to mind satin trim on a blanket worn to a nub by a small girl's fingers.

In my earliest memory, I am three years old and lying in a hospital crib, a satin blanket bunched in my hand. In the moonlight, the railings on my crib make shadows like prison bars across the floor. The wind punches the hospital's walls with winter's wallop. The old building groans with each jab. Tree branches scratch the windows with prickly fingers.

I'm too worn out from rheumatic fever to wonder why my mother is slumped in a chair in a dark corner. Her housedress rides up her splayed legs; a rosary is threaded through her fingers, and a hankie twisted in a damp knot lies on her lap. Her eyes are closed, her jaw slack. Her breathing is shallow as if she is on the edge of sleep. But I am not frightened by my mother's weariness or by the dark and the wind. I am detached from my surroundings, indifferent to what's happening as if this night belongs to another little girl.

In my mother's memory, she pummels a doctor's shoulder with her fists screaming, "You're letting her die! You're letting her die!" while he watches me convulse on an examination table, my eyes rolled back, drool pooling in the corners of my mouth. Three years later, certain that he saved my life, she will name my baby brother, Kevin, after this doctor. But for now, my father wraps his arms around her to contain her anger and fear.

In my siblings' memory, they kneel at dusk behind the chicken coop, coaxed into action by my sister's dramatic sensibilities. Perhaps the sting of the wind against their faces causes the tears to rise, or maybe the tears come from scraping a tin can's rusty lid against the goose-pimpled flesh of their arms, a shallow cut that leaves a ribbon of red trailing over their skin. Having heard the whispers, they offer blood for a little sister they fear may not live through the night.

But those are not my memories. Mine are of damp hair clinging to my face, a mouth dry as cottonwood fluff, and a square of felt on a braided chain scratching my chest. I wore a scapular with the image of Our Lady of Mount Carmel, the saint of maternal intercession, woven into the cloth. I rubbed the felt so often against my bottom lip those days that I drew blood. There is the smell of rubbing alcohol and bleach, and the crackling of cotton and a woman in white coming into the room. Something lures me from my bed, and I spiral downward into a dark yet safe place, perhaps our storm shelter cut into the hillside on a farm so distant from this crib I can't imagine having the strength to make the journey home. I long to sleep.

I wake to cool water on my forehead and to my mother's face pale in the moon's glow, a bottle of holy water shaped like the Blessed Virgin in one hand, and, in the other, a crucifix. She wraps my fingers around the Blessed Virgin, pins the crucifix to my pillow, and pulls a small vial from her pocket. Something warm drizzles over my bare skin, and I feel butterfly wings tracing the sign of the cross through the oil on my chest.

The woman shakes her head, "*Anyo*," when I slip the butterfly *maedeup* over a button on my coat. She thumbs through the pages of an illustrated book until she finds a picture of a lacquered cabinet. Then she drapes the ornament next to the picture to show how this *maedeup* is used to decorate furniture. I buy the butterfly, and when I am home, I drape it over a filigree knob on my antique wardrobe. It promises intimacy and abundance in our marriage, forgiveness and redemption in our lives.

She sets a tray of smaller ornaments on the counter, writes *norigae* on the slip of paper, and says something I do not understand. She is telling me the ornaments are *norigae*, decorative tassels from the Joseon period worn on the breast ties and belts of women in the ruling class. The women tied knots in the shapes of their hopes and fears— a pair of ducks for marital love, fish to ward off misfortune, cicadas for reincarnation, and pomegranates filled with seeds to symbolize a woman's hope for a son. Before I leave Korea, Dr. Han will give me a different amulet—a *norigae* with a bell-shaped piece of jade attached to a braided chain. Etched in the jade is a chrysanthemum, the symbol of a long and healthy life.

Among the many *norigae* my mother tied was a tiger claw that harnessed the tiger's power to protect her little girl, a turtle for endurance and resilience, and the image of a mother who drew me to her breast as if her heart might beat for both of us.

In a faded black-and-white photo, my mother wraps her arms around my legs, clasps her hands beneath my bottom, and pulls me to her chest. The picture taken in front of my Grandmother McManus' house is the only picture I have of just my mother and me. Mother is still a slender woman wearing a blouse with a notched collar and mother-of-pearl buttons. Her gathered skirt seems to flutter in the breeze, but her clunky shoes anchor her to the ground. Her hair is pulled away from her heart-shaped face and elongates her neck. She scrunches her nose and peers at the camera through wire-rimmed glasses. Something in the way her shoulders slump and her hip sags to the right suggests the weariness she will feel in the days of my illness yet to come. But the set of her jaw and her steady eyes hint at the determination that will sustain her.

My hair is wispy and the breeze lifts it from my scalp in fringes. Although I look pale, my cheeks and arms are chubby, but my calves are thin, and my dress hangs loosely from my shoulders. I lean into Mother, but tilt my head away, thumb in mouth, other hand behind her neck, clutching her hair or her blouse. The way I stare with nervous eyes at someone who is standing to the left of the photographer suggests the anxiety that lay beneath my contentment for most of my life.

The photo must have been taken in early summer because neither of us wears a jacket, and the bridal veil bushes that hug the foundation are lush. In the background are clumps of hollyhocks, whose blossoms I used to make dolls on Sunday afternoons when I sat cross-legged on my grandma's bed in a room that smelled of cold cream and dried flowers in a cut-glass bowl. I threaded the stamen through the opening in the flower and then turned the flower upside down so the petals became the skirt and the pistil the woman's yellow hair. When it was time to go home, the chenille bedspread was covered in pink petals and yellow stains.

For nine months after my bout with rheumatic fever, I was not allowed to walk or cry for fear of weakening my heart. I was confined to my crib or the living room sofa, on warm days to a makeshift bed in the shade of the back porch, and to my grandmother's bed on Sunday afternoons when the family gathered after mass for dinner.

Sitting on her bed, sorting through the hollyhocks, I listened to the sounds of my family. The screaming of siblings and cousins as they threw a ball over the roof, caught it, and then chased one another around the house. I imagined the girls' skirts twisting around their legs as they ran, their hair flying behind them, and the boys' shirttails flapping as they kicked up dust with their best shoes. I heard my father and uncles talking and smoking cigarettes near the shed in the backyard. I wonder now if it was beer they poured into their coffee mugs, their eyes on the kitchen window where my mother and aunts, in aprons and with scarves tied around their hair, chatted and laughed as they fried chicken, squeezed lemons, and cut pieces of cake and slices of pie. I am sure that I wasn't left by myself in that bedroom for more than a few minutes at a time. But there are moments even now when I am surrounded by family that I feel very much alone.

In tying *maedeup,* the weaver controls each step from teasing out the silk strands, intertwining them into a single *sul,* and then braiding it into a knot. This final step is the most critical, for if the thread is not properly tied, the knot is loose and distorted and will eventually come undone.

In the days of my illness, my mother was chained by fear that brought her running to my crib every time I moaned or coughed and made her call the doctor with every flush that crept over my cheeks. How did she endure those days? She had three other children, all under the age of ten, and hours filled with chores.

Mondays, she threaded clothing heavy with water through wringers, lugged baskets to the clothesline, then sprinkled shirts and dresses with water and curled them into balls she tucked in the clothes basket. Tuesdays were ironing day, with Arthur Godfrey on the radio as she pressed the iron against cotton and denim, steam dampening her face. Fridays, she scrubbed floors until her knees were red and calloused. Every day was a day to cook three meals and two lunches for my father, to bake bread and pies and cakes, pluck chickens, and husk corn. Nights were spent leaning over my crib, her hand against my forehead, her fingers pulling the blanket up around my shoulders.

Saturdays, she carried me or pushed me in a stroller through the stores where she shopped for thread and needles, shoes and sweaters for her children. I was too young to understand why people looked with curiosity and pity at a three-year-old who didn't walk. Why they bent over to stroke my hair or to pat my arm. One day, I recognized disgust in their eyes as I screamed and pointed to a doll with curly hair, pink cheeks, and blue eyes that opened and closed. I clutched the doll as my mother furiously pushed the stroller out of the store, my bones jiggling in tandem with the wheels rattling over the concrete. A woman had chastised Mother for spoiling me, saying that her own child had suffered from rheumatic fever as well and she didn't baby her. Years later, Mother's voice still quivered when she said, "What did she know about it, anyway? I was just doing everything I could to make you well."

As my health improved, I became restless and demanding. I knelt in my crib coloring, on the wallpaper. I chewed on the railings, leaving railroad tracks in the wood. I tossed toys and paper dolls out of the crib and hollered "Somebody aintain me." My mother snapped her fingers, and one of my siblings came into my room and slouched in the chair as they read books to me. Sometimes I made them play cowboys and gallop my plastic palomino around the corral of my crib. "Giddyup, Trigger," I hollered. "Giddyup." Once, my ten-year-old brother, Jim—probably tired of my games—lifted me from my crib and let me stand at the window to watch my father work in the yard. When my mother came into the room, she whisked me up, put me back in bed, and, in his words, "gave him holy hell for being so irresponsible." My siblings must have been tied in knots of resentment and guilt.

One day, I stood bare-chested in front of a piece of glass while a nurse held my hand. The doctor stood by a large machine. There was the sensation of something cold against my bare skin and a clicking sound. The film held to a light revealed no abnormalities in my organs. But even then, tiny traces of strep were invading my right kidney and eating away at the muscle and flesh.

I sat on Mother's lap as the doctor put a stethoscope to my chest and my back. "Take deep breaths," he said. Hearing no sluggish or irregular heartbeat, he gave me permission to walk again. Mother put me down and let go of my hand. I collapsed. Mother cried. This was the pattern of our days, I am told. I wobbled and fell, and Mother cried. Then one day, I don't know why, perhaps a mother's intuition, she put me down, walked to the other side of the room, knelt, and held out her hands. I took a step, stopped, looked with surprise at my skinny legs, took another step, then another. Finally, I tottered across the room, my fingers reaching to grasp her outstretched hands.

There are three elements in decorative knots— kkeunmok, the cord or thread, sul, the tassels, and maedeup, the knot. My mother and I were triangulated by the threads she used to connect us, beginning with the cord that nourished me in her womb. Then she tied the filaments of my fragile heart into a knot that has held for sixty years. And finally a maedeup so tight, I clung to her in fear that without her hand holding mine, I would lose my balance. But such a knot cannot hold, for daughters will eventually strain against their mothers' ties. So my mother, that master weaver, tied a double-clinch knot that braids two separate strands into a *maedeup* that grows stronger with each tug.

I have braided my *maedeup* in the shape of hands—my mother's hand on my feverish forehead as I tossed in my hospital bed; hands pulling the blanket over my shoulders as I recovered from a surgery to remove a kidney; her knotted fingers weaving the air in her hospice bed and murmuring words I couldn't understand, but hoped were defiant arguments with death; her hand in mine, her heart beating softly—like the fluttering of wings—until it stopped.

Chapter Four

When I walk up the stairs to my office for my first conference with Gil, I find him pacing the hall. He sees me, stops, bows, and says, "I was nervous, but you walk like this." He pumps his arms and strides down the hall. "I relax because you are energetic and will understand youth."

Of all my students, Gil is the most entrenched in Confucian tradition. He always stands by my door waiting for me to invite him to come in, bows, and steps into my office. He bows again before sitting down. He once asked, "Can I come in room without bowing?" I told him of course. But he could not give up the custom of bowing in deference to his teacher.

He brings me bookmarks, tasseled ornaments for my cell phone, cups of coffee, and flowers. As we talk, he leans forward, elbows on his knees, his palms open. "Am I saying that right?" he asks. He rarely looks me in the eye because it is bad manners to maintain eye contact for too long and especially disrespectful for a student to look directly into his teacher's eyes. I try to respect that custom, but it frustrates me. I have always relied on seeing my students' eyes to detect a cloud of confusion or the light of understanding.

In Confucian tradition, Gill tells me, students seek a teacher to guide their studies. "I picked you because I want to join the literary class. I think that is honorable scholarship because stories so important."

I am flattered to be included in the ancient Korean tradition of scholars mentoring students, but uncertain of my ability to live up to his expectations.

It was in Neo-Confucian *yangbang* settlements like Hahoe, the Joseon Dynasty Village in the North Gyeongsangbuk Province, where students learned from scholars, a tradition that still guides the choices Gil makes. In Hahoe, the past—thatched roof structures where scholars once met—collides with the present, post-and-beam homes with satellite dishes perched on mud-brick walls.

41

There is an immediacy of earth in this place—in the feathery ginkgo trees blanketing the houses, the rice fields unfolding over the plains, and the Nakdong River winding around the village. Time seems to tarry here like two school boys who trudge along the path, stop to stare at foreigners in their village, and then move on. They slide the toes of their shoes through the dirt, leaving narrow tracks behind them.

I wander through a courtyard between *jeongasas,* rooms where young men from the landed gentry met to study poetry and calligraphy. They were taught by *seonsaengs* wearing horse hair *kats* and ramie robes cinched at their waists. It was the job of these teachers to prepare young men for the imperial examination that identified those with the mettle to work in civil service, the most prestigious career at that time.

I linger in a tiny room with wooden beams and paper doors. I imagine the ghosts of students sitting on the floor chewing on their braids as they take the exam, dipping pens into ink pots, and making swooping lines on paper. Test-takers were often sequestered in scorching cells for seventy hours with little or no water. Some did not survive. In the wind rustling the leaves on ginko trees is the wailing of mothers as the bodies of their sons are carried back to them on boards.

There are ghosts in my hometown, Reliance, South Dakota. Like Hahoe, there is the feeling of a place where time has stopped. The St. Mary's Social Hall has been demolished and Henry's Grocery boarded up. At night Main Street is dark, except for the light coming from the saloon or from the glitter of gravel in the headlights of an occasional car. In the schoolyard, grasses push up through the gravel to reclaim old ground. It is a place that anchors me still even though I left here years ago.

The autumn I entered first grade, my father loaded my mother's upright piano onto the back of a cattle truck and moved us to a town on the east bluffs of the Missouri River. One story is that he wanted us to live in town because he believed the school offered the courses we needed for college. But we moved after the blizzard of 1949. That story includes a father who drove eight miles through the blizzard to pick up his children from school. On the way home, the jeep swerved into a pile of deep snow and was stuck. I always imagine the snow around the headlights, incan- descent in their glow. He dragged and carried my brothers and sister through the storm back to the house, vowing never again to put his children in such danger. A few hours later, the road leading to the farm was buried in snow, leaving us stranded for six weeks. But I am too young for that memory. I remember the drifts piled up to the roof of the garage and a plane buzzing overhead. The pilot dropped bags that contained yeast, sacks of flour, and a bundle of comic books. I remember the silence as the bags floated toward the ground and then my mother's tears when the bags broke and yeast peppered the snow.

As we hauled our belongings into the boxy, two-story house on the lip of a river gully, neighbors peeked behind curtains, and townspeople drove by slowly. Finally, the man across the street came over and said, "I never heard of a farmer moving into town."

I often wonder if our old neighbors believed we had deserted our little school and the community. Perhaps not. We were only five children among an exodus of young people that has plagued the Great Plains since the days of settlement, a tale of leaving home told over and over, a story of schoolhouses shedding boards and bricks like birds molting feathers.

Gil's scholarly ambitions began in sixth grade when he prepared for the college exam. "I attended after-school *hagwon* (a private academy), then studied at home until midnight. Going to *hagwon* is important to score well on the college exam," he says.

Attending a *hagwon* is a status symbol among Korean students, something like designer jeans or smart phones for American teens. The Korean government estimates there are ninety-five thousand *hagwons* in Korea employing eighty-four thousand private tutors. The tuition is very expensive and many fathers work two jobs to pay for their children's studies. Worried about the financial burden on families, as well as the stress on children, the government now restricts the hours a *hagwon* can be open. This has sparked a new class of professionals—*hagparazzi*, whistle blowers who spy on and report those who violate these restrictions. Some whistleblowers earn as much as one hundred thousand dollars a year.

Still, the private academies are a booming business. In late afternoons, we often saw children spill out of city buses and trudge down the sidewalk to the *hagwons*. Their backs were bent by the weight of the books they carried in their knapsacks and by the expectations of parents and their nation.

Gil tugs at his long bangs and thinks for a moment before saying, "In fifth grade, we worry about failing the test and disappointing our families and our country. Too much stress on children."

I thought of the April afternoon we wandered through a park in Gyeongju. School kids on motorized three-wheelers whizzed by us, screaming and laughing and crowding us off the sidewalk, uncharacteristically wild for Korean children who were generally well behaved. We asked the concierge about the children. He said that schools send fifth graders on field trips "because it's their last chance to be young and have fun before they study for exam. From now on, life will be difficult for them."

"Could the state education department use a different exam, something like the ACT that American students take?" I ask Gil.

"*Aniyo.* Big problem. The education department too *keun,* what is word I want?" He stretches his long arms above his head and makes a wide circle.

"Big? Large?"

"*Ye,* too big to change. There is too much tradition." He shrugs his shoulders. "Nothing to be done."

Gil gazes out the window at the mountains shrouded in smog. "My father works in a factory all day and drive taxi at night to pay for my education, you see. This is a great sacrifice for him. I have to succeed in school to repay his sacrifice."

Gil and I both grew up with fathers who made sacrifices for our education, but Gil's sacrifice overwhelms me. I was an indifferent college student spending more time at keg parties than at my studies. Despite my mediocre grades in every subject but English, my father continued to fund my education and said little about my poor performance. Confucius taught that when parents die, their children should fulfill the goals their parents once imagined for them. Three years after my father's death, I went to graduate school and received all As. I finally earned my father's patience, a gift I cherish and a burden I still carry.

The next time we take a taxi, I pretend it is Gil's father who stops for us. I see Gil's shock of black hair streaked with silver, his elegant hands on the wheel. The cab driver glances at the index card I give him, reads the address Miss Kim copied in Hangul, and eases the taxi away from the curb. An air freshener swaying from the mirror smells of pine, and there is hint of spice in his aftershave. His white gloves and face are pale in the light of the dashboard dials. He wraps his hand around a steering wheel knob and weaves the taxi through the traffic, his eyes focused on the road ahead of him. The cab is quiet, except for the whining of tires against pavement. Because Confucius did not have a concept of heaven, he found sacred places in the material world, like the ancestor tables in homes and the academies of learning. I find a sacred space in this hushed cab and in the fields my father worked.

For nearly twenty years, my father rose early to attend mass, sometimes waking me up to go with him. He knelt in the pew, his eyes lifted to the crucifix above the altar, his lips moving but making no sound. After mass, he slid into his pickup, where our black lab, Nipper, usually waited, and drove the bridge over the river, his yellow chamois gloves stretching at the seams as he gripped the steering wheel.

He spent his days looping a field on a tractor with only a canvas umbrella to shield his face from the sun and no cab to stop the wind. He planted his dreams for us the way he planted the seeds that would break through the sod in the spring. At the end of the day, he crossed back over the river, ate supper, smoked a cigarette as he read a book, and then knelt by his bed, a rosary threaded through his calloused fingers. Was this the life he once imagined?

My father, Henry John Woster, was the grandchild of immigrants from the vanished countries of Moravia and Bohemia. He inherited the restless feet of those who can claim no homeland. He graduated high school during the Dust Bowl, when work on the farm had dried up like the creek that meandered through the draw. He rode the rails with other hobos to the Chicago World's Fair, where he slept in a flophouse for twenty-five cents a night. I don't remember my father telling stories about his adventure. Did he tour the Hall of Science or the Shedd Aquarium? Did he eat spumoni at Lessa's Café in the Italian Pavilion? Drink pilsner in a beer garden? I like to think that he slipped into the tent to watch Sally Rand sashay across the stage behind her feathery fans, dipping them ever so slightly to his delight.

When he returned from Chicago, he hitchhiked to the Black Hills, hoping to find work at Homestake Gold Mine. But he learned his mother was going blind, so he came home and took a job driving the school bus. He spent the days reading in Father Reilly's library at the St. Mary's Rectory.

"Your dad is a self-taught man," my mother bragged. "He read every single book on those shelves."

The library of a small-town priest was surely small, and my father's achievement likely less impressive than my mother believed. But I like to imagine my father in that study, an earnest young man with pale blue eyes behind wire-rim glasses, a man thirsting for the knowledge contained in the books he held in his broad hands. What were his dreams? Of living in the city? Of being a scholar or perhaps a priest? Was it in that little library that he abandoned his own ambitions and planned the sacrifices he would make to give his children an education?

Mother, too, made sacrifices—she never owned a diamond ring or a fur coat, and her house was small and modest. But I can't imagine her making the sacrifices that many Korean mothers, nicknamed "education mommas," make. I read of one mother who rode a bus to the temple where she bowed, knelt, pressed her forehead to the floor, and then repeated the process two thousand times as an offering for her son's success. I imagined her later that night hovering over her little boy in his bedroom as he studied at his desk, nudging his shoulder to wake him up when his head nodded. Did she ever long to rest her hand on his silky hair for just a moment, to gather him in her arms and carry him to his bed?

Mother would never have hovered over me as I studied or huddle on cold tile beneath the crucifix. Mother lived life as if good food and lively music were all her children needed. She spent her days circling the kitchen between the mixer and the stove, leaving often to sit at the piano, her fingers weaving notes and keys into music she heard in her head. She negotiated conflicts between her children while she played. She bandaged bleeding fingers with one hand, sifted flour with the other. In the same way she improvised her music, she improvised her life without losing a beat in the melody of her days.

Near the end of the semester, Gil comes to my office and, with a deep bow, presents a bouquet of pink carnations wrapped in netting and tied with a satin bow. "I have something serious to say today."

He plunks down in the chair, props his elbow on the armrest, and cups his chin in his long fingers. "I want badly to study in America, but I feel guilt for wanting to leave and sorrowful, too, because I am eldest son and so have big responsibility to care for my parents. What would you do?"

I think hard for a moment before I answer Gil's question.

"I would be speaking as a person from the West, not the East, and as a daughter, not a son," I finally say. "I don't want to contradict Korean culture or your parents' wishes."

He is polite, but firm. "I am not asking about western or Korean values. I am asking for an honest answer. What would you do?"

How could I lie to this young man? "I would follow my heart."

I was among my siblings and several cousins who followed our hearts and left home to attend the university, following the path my Uncle George charted years before. In my favorite photo of Uncle George he is a scrawny boy in a wool suit and stiff white collar. He looks at the camera with intelligent eyes and an impish grin.

My mother often told the story of my uncle who frightened the neighbors when he was a boy by tromping the pastures with a homemade radio in one hand and a long piece of wire in the other, stopping to lift the wire over his head and make slow circles in the grass.

"But your Grandfather McManus always said 'that boy isn't crazy, he's just too brilliant for this place.'" That was the theme of my childhood. If you're bright or creative, you must leave.

When Uncle George announced that he wanted to attend Kansas State University to study aeronautical engineering, my Grandfather Woster—whom I know only from pictures as a stern-looking man with small eyes and rigid jaw—flew into a rage and vowed to disinherit his son if he left the farm. My father must have been around twelve when the battle between his brother and father erupted. Did he cower in a corner, listening to angry words? Did fear loosen my father's small hands on his dreams? Did he grieve as he watched his older brother leave for college?

I once asked my mother why my grandfather objected to George pursuing a college education. "Oh, I don't know, I think he was just mean," a judgment clouded perhaps by the fact that her in-laws intimidated her with their strange tongue and foods she considered inedible. But Grandpa Woster was the child of parents who left their family and homeland to pursue the dream of owning their own land.

Did George's desire to leave that land seem like a rejection of the sacrifice they had made? As he watched his oldest son leave the farm, did sorrow cross the boundary into anger as it so often does? According to my mother, my grandfather was a man of his words, and Uncle George learned at the reading of the will that he was left nothing.

Uncle George spent his career working as an engineer for Hughes Aircraft in Kansas City. He came back to the farm every summer with his wife and five children in tow. In my mind's eye, he strides through the north pasture, hands clasped behind his back, floppy hat pulled down to his ears, and shirttail coming loose from his waistband. I always imagine him kneeling to pick up a handful of soil and watching it sift between his sinuous fingers. I always wonder if he saw loss or salvation in the soil slipping back to the earth.

"Sad today?" Gil asks.

It is our last conference, and I stand at the window looking at the haze that smothers the mountains. Below me, men and women wearing surgical masks scurry down the crowded sidewalks through a yellow curtain of dust draped over the campus. In a nearby park, children spin on merry-go-rounds, their shouts muffled behind masks stamped with Dora the Explorer and Mickey Mouse.

The night I arrived in Korea, I assumed people wore masks to avoid infection. I later learn that the masks protect their lungs from the yellow dust, *hwangsa*, that blows across the Yellow Sea from the arid regions of Northern China, Inner Mongolia, and Manchuria. In the mornings, our cabinets and desks would often be covered in a layer of fine yellow sand.

I suddenly feel claustrophobic and relieved that I will soon be going home where I can see the horizon without the interruption of mountains or haze.

"Oh, Gil," I say. "I wish you could see the South Dakota sky. It's a dome painted in seven shades of blue, and it stretches forever. I miss it so much."

He nods his head as if he understands, but the wrinkles in the corners of his eyes betray him. How could this young man who knows mostly the compression of buildings and mountains and the weight of smog understand such a landscape?

He sits in his chair and waits for a moment before speaking. In the sunlight Gil's hair is raven-black, his face youthful. But his eyes are weary. He tugs at his bangs and studies the streaks in the tile on my office floor as if they hide the words he needs.

"I must stay in Korea and be best student I can be, then find good job so my parents can live with me in their old age. It will be very hard, but that is my obligation."

Gil was grounded in the Confucian traditions, in the rituals he would one day perform before the ancestor altar, and the values he would pass on to his children. I sympathize with his feeling the burden of this responsibility. Yet I envy him that he will always be sustained by his past.

When our conference ends, I give Gil a book of paintings by South Dakota artist Harvey Dunn, who depicts his childhood homestead on the prairie—the man steering a plow behind an oxen, the woman picking wildflowers. I want to give Gil a hug, but I am afraid that would offend his Confucian sensibilities. He bows. "You taught me much this semester. *Kamsahmnida.*"

He walks toward the door, then stops and turns. He smiles and bows one last time. "I hope for blue skies when you are home in South Dakota. Then you be finding happy."

Back in Brookings, I sit at my computer, revising the same sentence over and over, fretting that writing a book is a futile effort. Chimes announce the arrival of an email. It is from Gil, our first correspondence since we left Korea. He writes, "I hope you can remember me from the faces of memory."

As I read his email, I hear his soft voice and see his serious brown eyes studying the floor for words. "I am writing my dissertation. Do you know, Professor, what I am writing about? Fairytales, rituals of primitives, and mythologies."

Gil and I had a ritual of swapping folk legends. I would tell him about Heyoka, the contrary character in Lakota tradition, and he related the story of Chung Kayguri, the green frog who went east when told to go west. Gil was fascinated with the overlap between Native American mythology and Korean folklore and curious how these legends could span centuries and continents to blend the same elements into different stories.

"I still young," he writes, "but sometimes, I wonder how we influence each other even after such a short time sharing stories."

I think of our last conference and my saying, "Gil, tell me one last folk tale."

He recounted the story of a boy and girl who ran up a tree to escape a tiger. "Then," he said, twisting his long bangs around a finger, "God let down a ladder and pulled the children into sky. The children became the sun and the moon."

I shared with him the Kiowa legend of seven sisters playing with their brother. The brother suddenly became a bear and chased the girls up a tree. The trunk rose up and up until finally the girls flew into the sky to become the stars of the Big Dipper.

I end the story saying, "And so, the Kiowa say as long as the legend lives, they will have relatives in the night sky."

We sat for several minutes in the comfortable silence of those whose affinity transcends words. Gil fiddled with his bangs, his eyes closed as he wove the threads of his thoughts into the question he needed to ask.

For the first time, he looked directly into my eyes. "So, Professor Mary, stories keep people alive forever?"

For a moment, I stared out the window. I couldn't speak. Finally, I looked at him and said, "Yes, I believe they do."

Chapter Five

"Whoever decided Adam and Eve were naked any-
way?" my mother asks as she bends over an illustrated Bible,
a fistful of my little brother's crayons in her hand.

This image emerges from the deep pools of memory
as I scrub myself in a Korean spa, surrounded by naked
women. As I remember it, Mother's hair is dark and wavy,
her body fleshy beneath a housedress printed with watering
cans and daisies. She furrows her eyebrows as she flips
through the pages. Their gilt-edges are showers of gold
flickering over the tabletop.

I am a girl in cutoff jeans and a crop top lying on my
stomach near her feet. I am reading a book and chewing on
my pony tail. The carpet is rough in patches and scratches
my tummy. When I squirm to find a comfortable position,
dust motes rise.

"Humph, look at this picture. How ridiculous."

I stand up, lean over her shoulder, and breathe in the
smell of talcum powder on her neck while she colors a red
dress on Eve, who lounges naked against a tree, an apple
in one hand and the fingers of the other hand spread over
her pelvis. Above her, a snake coils around a tree branch
and weaves through the leaves, its tongue flittering toward
Eve's hair. On a mission to clothe more women, Mother
riffles through the pages. She scribbles a green dress on
Bathsheba stepping out of a pool of water, paints a brown
camisole in the plunging neckline of Delilah's silky gown,
and puts a pair of purple slacks on Abisag's bare buttocks.

Around me nude women dangled their feet in the
water as they nurse their babies or meander around the
pools brushing their teeth or nibbling on slices of apple
they cut with knives. One backstrokes in water so shallow
her bottom nearly scrapes the concrete. Another leans into
a mirror, her bare breasts against the glass as she applies
eyeliner and mascara. So many naked women that even with
a forty-eight-box of crayons in hand, my mother could not
possibly clothe them all.

*　　*　　*

I come from a family so modest we dressed in closets or the bathroom, so I am glad none of them are watching as I walk up the stairs at the Boryeong Mud Spa, take off my shoes, set them on a wooden mat outside the door, and buy a ticket for four hundred *won* (about four dollars) from the attendant.

Earlier that day, Ken jumped over the black rocks that lined Muchangpo Beach, which is a few hours southwest of Daejeon. I lagged behind him, doing the two-step over the hair net of moss that covered the rocks. We came to this beach as guests of Dr. Nho to witness the Miracle of Moses, a natural phenomenon that happens when the pull of the moon causes the tides to retreat and opens a path to an island almost a mile offshore. People wearing slickers scraped clams off the exposed rocks and dropped them into buckets, along with clumps of seaweed. Children in yellow boots squatted near the rocks, looking for sea creatures in the tidal pools.

We leave Muchangpo and drive to the seaside town of Boryeong, famous for its beaches and the restorative power of its mud. Dr. Nho leads us to a restaurant housed in a tent that specializes in *jogae gui*, grilled shellfish. The wind is chilly, and the canvas tent flaps against fish tanks where oysters, clams, and mussels disguise themselves in the rocks. We hurry to grab a table near a gas heater. The waiter brings *miyuk gook*, seaweed soup; *bap*, rice; *yangnyum ganjang*, seasoned soy sauce mixed with *ggae*, toasted sesame seeds; and a platter of shellfish. A handsome man who hates having his picture taken, Ken smiles easily at the camera as he flips clams and oysters on a charcoal grill built into the tabletop. When the shells sizzle and yawn, releasing puffs of steam, we put on white gloves and pry the shells open with pliers. As I slurp the flesh from the husks, hot water runs down my sleeve. The smell of salt soaks into my skin.

After lunch, Dr. Nho suggests we visit the mud spa. We walk into a large building of concrete and glass. In the foyer, photos of the annual Boryeong Mud Festival hang on the wall. There are pictures of men and women relaxing in mud bathtubs, sliding down a mud slide, and wrestling and playing softball in the mud. One of the photos shows the winners of the Mr. Mud and Ms. Mud contest wearing mud crowns and mud bathing suits. I am surprised at the sensuousness of these photos, a contrast to Dr. Nho's restrained Confucian demeanor. I wonder why he brought us here.

"Should we try the baths for the experience?" he asks.

I tug at the back of Ken's jacket, a signal that he should decline the invitation. But he asks, "So are the baths separated by gender?"

"Of course. There will only be men in our bath and women in Mary's."

"That sounds great," Ken says.

Ken was always more comfortable with his body than I. The morning after we were married, I walked into the bathroom to find him shaving naked in front of the mirror. "Good morning," he said. I was stunned. What kind of man stands naked in front of a mirror? What kind of man had I married? I had never seen my father wearing less than a white cotton t-shirt and gray work pants. Unlike me, Ken easily immersed himself into the bath culture.

Nor did the women in my family walk around in our underwear like my friend's mother, who scrubbed the floor and dusted the furniture wearing a pointy bra and silky panties. I only glimpsed my mother's underwear on the clothesline, usually flapping in the wind behind the sheets or my father's coveralls. Her undergarments were a mystery to me. One day when I was little, I crept into her bedroom, pulled out a bra, hooked the snaps, and pulled it up by the straps over my shoulders. I couldn't imagine the day I would fill out the cups that dangled like upside-down parachutes against my flat chest.

I have never been comfortable being undressed in front of others, even women. In high school I lied to my gym teacher at least twice a month, saying I had a visit from my 'friend,' just to avoid showering after class. In college, I crept into the bathroom stalls after gym class and waited for the room to empty before I changed out of my orange bloomers into a skirt and sweater and dashed off late to class. It would be many years after our marriage before I finally left the lights on when I undressed.

My mother's voice interrupts my thoughts. *Are you nuts? You're going to be nude in a public place?"*

But also I hear my own voice saying, "Ken, let's promise that we are going to accept every invitation to experience Korean culture." I had already kept my promise the day a little boy named John looked at the dried fish, eyes and scales intact, lying at the bottom of my metal bowl and asked, "Don't you like our fish?" I grappled the fish between my chopsticks, popped it into my mouth, chewed, swallowed, and mentally crossed eating silver-scaled fish off my cultural to-do list. In that same spirit, I walked into the bath.

The attendant gives me an expandable bracelet with a metal disc and points to several rows of lockers. After wandering a bit, relieved I am the only one in the room, I find my locker, but I can't open the door. I am fumbling with the bracelet when the attendant comes around the corner, grabs my wrist, and holds the disc to the lock, which makes a grinding noise and then pops the door open. She gestures that I should take off my clothes and put them in the locker.

I take off my jeans, then my socks, and finally my turtleneck sweater, folding and stacking them in a tidy pile in the cubbyhole. Then she points at my bra and panties and again at the locker. I shake my head "no," hoping that she will let me wear my underwear in the bath.

What are you thinking? I hear my mother say.

I am willing to ride home in wet and muddy underwear rather than answer Mother's question.

The woman stands her ground, glaring at me with her hands on her hips.

Then she reaches over and tugs at my panties, muttering and pointing at the locker. Finally while she stands just inches away, I take off my undies and throw them in the cubbyhole. She hands me a towel the size of a newborn's diaper and points to a door on the opposite side of the room, a distance I estimate to be four hundred yards, although as I consider it now, more likely forty feet.

Mustering my dignity, I straighten my back and shoulders, clutch the towel to my middle somewhere between breast and pubic bone, and walk across the room to enter the bath, feeling the attendant's eyes on my bare back.

Previous exchange professors had told us that Koreans scrub themselves meticulously before entering the baths, which seems pointless in a mud spa. Erring on the side of caution, however, I enter a shower stall, pick up a rough scrubbing cloth and a bar of soap from the shelf, and turn on the water. I quickly run the cloth up one side of my body and down the other, shampoo my hair, rinse, and scurry into the misty spa, wanting to get into the water before other women come into the room.

There is a large pool with gently rolling waves and a sign in English that reads: "Seawater Pool." I walk down two steps into the water, thinking that because it is the largest pool, it will also be the deepest. But the water only reaches my knees. As I sit at the edge of the pool, bubbles caressing my feet, I can hear water gurgling, steam pipes hissing, and a lazy plopping sound like a Yellowstone mud pot. I peer through the steam and see a pool of muddy water and a long wooden tray filled with mud.

Oh, why not?

I walk over to the tray, smear the pasty mud over my body, and sit on the pool's edge for several minutes, feeling my skin pucker as the mud dries. Then I slide into the tub. The water is mucky looking, but silky against bare skin. I just begin to relax when I hear her voice once more. *Oh, for the love of Mike, have you lost your mind? Only pigs wallow in mud.*

As we drive home that night, I am glad I can cross going to the baths off my list, and I am certain I will never go back. I am also relieved I won't hear my incredulous mother's voice ever again.

The next class period, I tell my students, "Well, guess what. I went to a mud spa this weekend." The women giggle behind their hands. The men duck their heads and grin.

"I have never been to a public bath before, and I probably won't go again. But I am happy I tried it."

Bora asks, "Don't you have baths in America?"

"We have spas," I say, "but I don't know of any public baths where everyone is naked."

"But you American women are more free than Korean women. American women wear sexy clothes and dance sexy."

I laugh. "Well, this American woman doesn't wear sexy clothes, and she's too stiff to swivel her hips and prance around the dance floor."

But I understand her confusion. These students have watched the exhibitionism of Britney, Paris, and Madonna on MTV, and they can't reconcile those images with a Western woman's professed modesty, no matter how old she is.

Even young women raised in a hyper-sexualized American culture are strangely more modest than my Korean students might have expected. During our time in Korea, several students from SDSU came over to tour the campus. At a university banquet, a couple of the women wore slinky gowns with necklines that plunged to their waists, yet when I asked them if they had tried the spa at the hotel, they flushed and stammered until finally one admitted, "We went to the bath last night, but we swore we wouldn't tell anybody back home. We don't want people to know we were naked in a room full of women."

I overheard one of the women whisper, "I'd rather be naked in front of a man than a woman." Good lord. What does that mean? Then I remembered how I had once hidden from other women in bathroom stalls.

In contrast, the shy Korean women in my English conversation class wear baggy t-shirts or blouses buttoned at the neck and loose fitting jeans or tights under short skirts. Once I had seen the baths where giggling girls jumped in and out of the water and sat next to their mothers dangling their feet in the pool, I understood their ease with nudity.

Bora insists I try the baths one more time. "I'll go with you to the Yuseong Hotel spa and show you how."

For the only time in Korea, I refuse an invitation. Anonymous nudity is one thing, nudity with a girl I'd have to face in class the next day, quite another. I now regret saying no. Bora might have taught the teacher a lesson, might have instilled in me a healthy attitude about my body. But overcoming sixty years of modesty was challenging enough. I wasn't prepared to reduce myself to the vulnerability of naked flesh in front of my student. However, she did convince a reluctant woman to try the baths one more time.

The next week at the Yuseong Hotel, I follow my routine of methodically removing each piece of clothing and folding it neatly. Then I cower behind the locker door for several minutes, clutching the tiny towel to my middle until I work up the courage to walk across the dressing room and past the beauty shop, where a stylist wearing only her underwear sits on a stool and cleans hairbrushes. I cross over to the door that leads to the baths.

I peer through the steamy window and see several women scouring themselves with rough cloths as they sit at the edge of a kidney-shaped pool. I remember visiting the Degas exhibit at the Chicago Institute of Art, where portraits of women bathing hung on the walls—slender and sinuous, stocky and sturdy women; blonde and fair-skinned, brunette and bronze. In the paintings they knelt or lay in shallow tubs, twisting their bodies in awkward, yet graceful, poses as they scrubbed or dried themselves with towels. In one painting, a woman lay on her side facing a copper bathtub, one leg lifted and resting on the tub's edge. A maid, in a blouse that ballooned above starched cuffs and a red skirt that billowed over the floor, lifted the woman's hair in one hand, and with the other dried her back. I marveled at the women's comfort with touching and being touched by one another.

In the time and place of my childhood, people were not often physically affectionate. I don't remember my parents or aunts and uncles embracing or kissing. Perhaps their reserve was the heritage of ancestors who grew up in repressive Old World churches that taught touch was sinful, lessons they packed in the trunks they carried to the Great Plains. I do remember watching my mother in front of a mirror as my father zipped up the back of her dress, a moment that thrilled me although I was too young to know why. One day I would feel the intimacy of a man's hands moving up my back and then resting on my shoulders as we looked at one another in the mirror. I wondered if, I hoped that, my mother felt the same way.

When I open the door, I hear loud *splats*, like the sound of my mother slapping bread dough on the counter. In the opposite corner, a masseuse in bra and panties uses her closed fists to pummel a naked woman's back. In another corner, several naked women nap on slatted wooden floors, their heads resting on rolled-up hand towels.

I walk across the room toward a scrubbing stool. Heads turn. My stomach tightens. I am an awkward seventh grade giant walking into the locker room after gym class, the eyes of tiny girls sitting on benches scrutinizing me. They were the girls who won the cheerleading elections and went home from basketball games with the starting guards, while we chunky girls crowded together in the bleachers, waving our pompoms and then went home alone. But the women return to their scrubbing and soaking, chatting quietly or gazing across the room. Westerners are still an oddity in much of Korea, and I may be the first naked Western woman they have ever seen. Perhaps they are simply curious.

As I soak in the bubbling water, I watch a young girl gently scrub the back of a frail, silver-haired woman too stiff to reach around and wash her own flesh. Then the old woman kneels at the edge of the pool for forty-five minutes as she scrubs herself, dipping a bowl into the pool and pouring the water over her head. There is something ancient about this old woman and her scrubbing, and I imagine her years ago leaving the children and the cooking pots, and the hut filled with smoke and grease. I imagine her gathering by a stream with other women, stripping off her filthy clothes, and wading into the cold water to sit on the pebbles that glitter beneath the surface, to scrub off the dirt and grime of her life. I have joined a venerable ritual practiced by women for centuries.

*   *   *

When my sister, Jeanne, comes to visit, we take the train to the resort town of Gyeongju, a popular tourist destination with hotels and spas lining the shores of Lake Bomun. Gyeongju, the capital city of the Silla Kingdom, sits in a wide basin enclosed by the Taebaek Mountains, the Yeongnam Alps, and the Hyeongsan River. Tucked in the trees on the hillsides is Bulguksa Temple, one of the most exquisite temples in South Korea. Seokguram Grotto is carved into the slopes of Tohamsa, the highest mountain in the coastal range east of the city. The grotto houses one of the largest statues of the Buddha in Korea.

I suggest we make separate reservations at the hotel spa. "Sorry, Jeanne, but I'm just not ready to be naked with you."

She laughs. "That's okay. I think we've shocked Mother enough already." *Those two girls don't have a lick of sense.*

So, we arrange to go to the baths at different times, preserving some measure of our family modesty.

Although I can't undress in front of my sister, I have come to relish the luxury of sitting on my stool in front of a mirror, free of shame or judgment as I tenderly scrub my bends and curves, freckles and dimples. Right after we check in, I hurry over to the baths. A chubby woman comes over, takes my hand, and leads me to a large pool with a pulsating waterfall. She stands under the waterfall with her head down while the jets of water batter her shoulders. Then she gestures to me and watches while I stand under the pounding water. She takes my hand again and guides me to a spot where water spurts just below the surface, turns her back, scrunches down, and moves her body back and forth through the streams. Once again, she watches as I imitate her. At another spot, she floats on her stomach and lets the churning water bounce her body in the bubbles. I do the same, riding the waves like a jellyfish. She pats my shoulder, says something I don't understand, and leaves. The next day when I return to the spa, she is soaking in the hot pool. We smile and wave like old neighbors greeting one another over the back fence.

I soak for a while, watching four young women on stools stare in mirrors as they scrub themselves, making small, slow circles over elbows, hands, legs, breasts, and neck. Their hair is gathered at the top of their heads and cascades in shiny black rivers down their necks. Their bodies curve in at their waists and out at their hips. Holding their arms

58

above their heads, they are dancers swaying to music only they can hear as they caress themselves with the cloths. With no sense of voyeurism, shame, or uneasiness, I watch them scrub for several minutes. Not even Degas had captured such beauty.

The outdoor pool nestles in a rock garden surrounded by a stone fence with purple and white hibiscus growing out of the cracks. I walk up steps to a patio with a bubbling hot pool. I soak for a bit and then sit at the pool's edge, feeling the sun warm on my bare back and the breeze against my breasts. Bees buzz around the perfume-laden flowers, and a cuckoo bird calls from rustling tree branches. Behind me a waterfall whooshes as it hits the pool below. Above me white clouds drift across a brilliant sky. A pollution-free day in Korea is rare, and I intend to enjoy it, even if it means ignoring my mother's command. *Are you crazy? Get back inside and put on your clothes.*

After a while, two women join me, naked except for small towels wrapped around their heads like turbans. They lie down on lounge chairs and chat as they sun themselves. What are they saying? Are they laughing about grand-children's antics or their husbands' foolishness? Are they sharing secrets of love affairs? Gossiping about neighbors and family?

I try to envision sitting naked with my friends as we talk about politics or books, but I can't.

When I return to South Dakota, I ask them, "If there were public baths in America, would you go to one with me?"

One woman says, "You mean in our swimsuits, right?"

"No, we'd be naked."

"Absolutely not. I'm not getting naked in front of anybody."

The rest of the women added qualifications.

"I'd probably go with my sister."

"Maybe if I had enough to drink."

I say, "I'd go if the spa were in another state and the room were full of women I'd never see again."

As I utter those words, I picture a painting of brown-skinned, dark-eyed, naked little girls, teenagers, young mothers, and old women soaking in pools, talking and laughing, sharing slices of apples, and scrubbing one another's bodies. At the edge of the painting, a gray-haired, pale, and heavy-breasted woman peers through a window. In Korea, I came to understand that scrubbing an old woman's back is an act of generosity, as is accepting the touch of another woman. I realized with sadness that the baths are a part of the life I have left behind in Korea.

I saw my mother naked for the first time when she was eighty-one years old. I wheeled her to her room at the nursing home where she was to begin rehabilitation after undergoing open heart surgery. An aide walked into her room and said, "We need to document Marie's condition on admission to make certain she doesn't have any bruises."

She slipped off Mother's clothes and dropped them on the floor. Mother stood by the twin bed, shivering, clothes in a pile around her feet, her withered body defenseless as a baby's. The aide circled her, checking off the items on a list in her hand like a rental car salesman looking for dents and scratches on a returned vehicle.

In that moment, my mother, who had guarded her modesty all her life, was defeated. She glanced at me and then turned her face to the wall. I bent over, picked up her clothes and underwear, slowly folded them, and put them in a neat pile on a chair by the bed. Then I fumbled in her overnight bag for her pajamas and handed them to the aide. I drove home that night weeping with regret and guilt that I had stood by and watched a stranger dress my frail mother.

I remember my tired, sick mother standing naked in a pool of her clothing. Had we been less inhibited in our family, I might retain a memory of her naked body during her younger years when power flowed through her heavy breasts, ample hips, and calves sturdy as fence posts. I try to envision caring for my mother the way Korean girls cared for the old women at the baths. Would she instinctively recoil at someone touching her naked flesh? Or would she relax into my hands scrubbing her back with a soft cloth? No doubt it was too late for such intimacy between us. Some patterns had been etched too deeply in our lives to be worn down by time or reworked by tears. Still I like to imagine my hands making small, tender circles over her fragile skin, my hands easing her dying.

Chapter Six

In my Irish Catholic family, there was no clear distinction between music and grace.

A young woman in a lemon linen blazer and silk trousers sits in front of a window that overlooks a valley as she plays "Danny Boy" on a *haegeum*. The quivering notes become cicadas trilling from tree branches on a farm nestled in grassland where a house smells of coffee and snickerdoodles; where cigarette smoke lingers in a room; and sepia-toned family photos, a crucifix, and a picture of Christ shellacked on barn wood clutter the walls. My mother sits at the piano, lifting her shoulders with each delicate arpeggio while my curly-headed Uncle Bill croons, "Tis I'll be here, in sunshine or in shadow, Oh, Danny boy, Oh Danny boy. I love you so." My aunties weep into their hankies, crystal rosaries wrapped around their fingers.

My Aunt Evelyn often told the story of the day my mother, only a toddler, crawled up on the piano bench, her stubby legs dangling over the floor, her wrists arched above the keys as she played "Tantum Ergo." When she was done, she hopped down and went outside to play with their collie, Rex, leaving her family a little woozy at this unexpected miracle. Other members of the family argued it was more likely something lively that the family liked to sing, perhaps "The Wearing of the Green," and that she sat on that bench for several minutes studying the keys before she slipped outside.

Was it by providence or by design that Mother's first communion picture was taken in front of that piano? She is a tiny bride in a dress with tiers of ruffles and a wreath of flowers circling her hair to keep her veil in place. The picture is taken at an angle, and the light shines down on the keys and the jeweled crucifix sitting on the piano top. My mother's body and face are washed out, and they merge into the piano's glow. She looks at the photographer out the corner of one eye with the expression of an old soul.

But what draws my eye is her hand holding back the veil. It seems outsized for a little girl. What unnerves me is the stillness of her fingers, usually so busy slicing and chopping meat and vegetables, cooling a child's feverish brow, pushing the stops on the church organ, flying over piano keys.

Nights with the Irish clan always ended with the benediction of her music. When I heard her fingers skipping over the bass notes that opened "Flight of the Bumblebee," I ran into the living room and knelt on the floor beneath the framed photos of my grandparents that sat on the top of the piano. Their eyes were lit by the garish green blobs that slogged through the gel of a lava lamp. I had no memory of my grandparents except for those photos, and as a child, I thought of them as eerie spirits, as if my mother had descended from the screaming banshees she warned me about. The more wildly Mother played, the more the frames inched toward the edge. Finally she hit a chord so ferocious it might have shattered glass. A photo toppled into my father's uplifted hands, and he extended it toward us like a gift.

We are touring the Korean Traditional Music Village, a complex of buildings with swallowtail roofs and murals of musicians in brightly colored uniforms marching across the exterior walls. Here artisans make traditional instruments and musicians teach children to play them. Here the ancient music is preserved.

We wander into a room where a man in work clothes and goggles stands in clouds of wood shavings as he planes the surface of an *ajaeng*, a seven-stringed instrument carved from a palowinia tree. Each stroke of metal against the wood releases the fragrance of forests that blends into an aroma of jasmine tea cooling in a ceramic bowl. He sits cross-legged on the floor, the bridge of the *ajaeng* overhanging his lap for several feet on either side. He runs his fingers over the wood, feeling for imperfections—a bump in the cylindrical sound box or a tiny hollow in the neck. He seems satisfied with his work. Still, he caresses the instrument once more with the touch of a lover memorizing the lines of his beloved's body.

In another room, the woman waits for us, a two-stringed *haegeum* with a short fret and drum-like bottom in one hand, a forsythia branch coated with resin in the other. Tied to the fret is a chocolate-brown *maedeup*. The tassels dance as she settles on the edge of a stool.

She smiles. "I am so pleased you have come to learn about our music. The first piece I am going to play is *sokak*, farm music three thousand years old. It was performed in villages where people danced to celebrate the harvest."

She bends over the instrument and draws the branch quickly across the strings. Her fingers dance over the frets, and she bobs her head to a beat like scythes slicing through wheat sheaves, or knives chopping at cabbage stalks.

"The next piece," she says, "is *jeongak*, or court music, our classical music. There is little melody, but mostly slow tones."

The tune is as mournful as wind sifting through pines, but there is a contented look on her face as she concentrates on pulling the branch slowly over the strings, sustaining each note longer than I thought possible. When she finishes, she says, "For a time, Koreans wanted to be modern and didn't care about old music or instruments. The trees and rivers remember, and so we must also."

"Do you have a song for me to play?" she asks.

"Danny Boy," says Ken. "That was Mary's family's favorite."

"Oh, yes, that's my father's favorite as well. You know that Irish priests brought this song to Korea when they came to establish missions. My father says the song expresses the soulful nature that Irish and Koreans share."

She closes her eyes and moves the bow slowly, her lithe body swaying with each note. The music is mournful and poignant and reminds me of strings reverberating off key when I plucked a loosely strung wire on my father's banjo and let it run through my pinched fingers.

The banjo was stored at the back of a walk-in closet next to my bedroom, along with a drum set, two accordions, and a tenor saxophone. When I was a small girl, I would sneak into the closet, past books stacked against the walls and under clothes that hung on a rack overhead. The sun shining through the window warmed the closet, which smelled of mothballs, talcum powder, dust, and crackled calfskin on drumheads.

I always felt as if I had stumbled upon a long-buried, sacred space like the catacombs or pyramids. Here I sifted through the relics of my parents' previous life—the instruments they played at Saturday dances before children and farm demanded their time; my father's double-breasted topcoat, a silk scarf tucked between the lapels; my mother's rose-colored dress with a sweetheart collar trimmed in yellowed lace; a felt fedora with a grosgrain band; and a cloche covered in pheasant feathers and rhinestones. Sometimes, I slipped the dress over my coveralls, plopped the hat on my tousled hair, and sat on the floor, fingering the keys on the sax or pumping the accordion's bellows and wondering about the farmer and the housewife who once wore these clothes. Could my parents have been that stylish and carefree?

If that space swaddled me in the sounds and smells of childhood, it also unsettled me. If my parents could abandon pieces of their former life, could they also abandon me? I was teetering on the edge of an epiphany that would cause a seismic shift in my innocence, an unarticulated awareness that time is fleeting, loss inevitable, and that one day the music of my childhood—like these old instruments—would be silenced.

Saint Patrick's Day in Gung Dong, I sit at a bar in Murphy's Irish Pub, sipping Hite beer and thinking how strange to spend this holiday in a place where neon signs blaze with advertisements for *tibidibang*, private movie rooms, *maekju*, beer, and *noraebang*, karaoke rooms; where wooden meat wagons line up on the curbs selling *ddeokbokgi*, skewered rice sticks soaked in a spicy red sauce; where, beneath a gilded statue of the Laughing Buddha, a young bartender tosses a martini shaker over his head, spins around, and catches it behind his back, all the while swiveling his narrow hips to the rhythm of Madonna blasting through the sound system.

Sitting next to me, a woman wraps her fingers around a Collins glass and sips something that smells of lemon and gin. She lifts a swizzle stick from the drink, pulls a maraschino cherry from its tip with her teeth, then nibbles as she studies her reflection in the mirror.

I gnaw on a string of dried squid and stare in the glass of another mirror where I am a college student in a piano bar called Charley's. The light tinges the flocked wallpaper and the whiskey bottles on the shelves in shades of burnished gold. My drink smells of vermouth and bitters, my wrists of Chanel No. 5. The men around me smell of mud and bloody feathers and whiskey. They are pheasant hunters who have flocked to South Dakota, where game birds often outnumber people. They slouch over the bar, elbows splayed, old fashioned glasses sweating between their fingers as they listen to my mother, who sits at a piano in a horseshoe bar.

Her eyes are closed, and a dreamy smile curves toward her cheeks as she bends over the piano and softly sings, "There's a queen waiting there, with a silvery crown, in a shanty in old shanty town." I look at the men, cigarettes dangling between their lips, smoke spiraling around their faces. Do they understand what they're seeing—this moment when a woman yields to the grace of music like a penitent in a dark confessional?

"Hey, how bout 'Santa Catalina,' Marie?" a droopy-eyed man hollers.

She shifts without missing a beat into the tune, and the men begin to sing, "Twenty-six miles across the sea," the words slurred from too many drinks and too many miles of trudging through cornfields in the cold winds.

When the bar closes, the men stagger to their motel rooms, and Mother comes home, her pocketbook jingling with change they tossed in a brandy snifter. As we count the coins and stack paper bills in piles, she tells stories of the hunters who gathered around the piano that night. My younger brother is thrilled to learn that the "big, jolly man with funny ears" is professional wrestler Verne Gagne. I'm tickled when she describes Yankee general manager Billy Martin as the "fidgety and flirty little fellow" who requested "Ramblin' Rose."

I don't know why Mother took a job playing the piano at Charley's during hunting season. She knew the owner well and perhaps he was looking for something to draw hunters to his motel and bar. I don't even know if she was paid more than tips. Probably not. As far as I know, she never earned a dime playing for funerals, weddings, parties at the nursing home, or the weekly Kiwanis Club meeting.

I still marvel that Mother, who despised cigarettes and booze—as so many Irish mothers do—would spend hours in a smoky lounge oblivious to the men growing more boisterous with each drink, their bantering with her ripe with innuendo. She was only fifty years old when my father died. Perhaps she missed the presence of a man, the smell of Old Spice, the broad hands wrapped around a wrench, and deep voices in the house, a gap these tipsy hunters may have filled. Or her music may have been an escape from her loneliness and the challenge of rearing a teenage boy. Most likely, she blocked out the smoke and the liquor because she craved an audience and because she had no choice but to entertain, although she would have denied this need. In most things, Mother was humble. "I just play the piano." But it was a false humility when it came to her music.

All her life, Mother relished leaving an audience astonished at the sight of her hummingbird fingers flittering over the keys as she improvised more fill notes and chords, tremolos and trills, arpeggios and accents than the composer might have imagined. People often compared her to Joanne Castle, the bleached-blonde, honky tonk pianist who wowed audiences in the early days of the Lawrence Welk show. But I knew they were looking through the wrong lens. Joanne Castle played like my mother.

When I was small, my mother's audience was not hunters, but her family; her stage, our living room. While the bread dough rose in her mixing bowl or the wax dried on the linoleum, she ran to the upright. She mostly played upbeat music, like "Maple Leaf Rag," "Chattanooga Choo Choo," and "Alexander's Ragtime Band," songs as familiar to me as nursery rhymes and bedtime prayers. One day in first grade, Miss Scott, whom I adored for her red skirt, chiffon blouse, and hankie fragrant with Evening in Paris perfume tucked into her bra, asked us to sing our favorite song. The other children sang "I'm a Little Teapot" and "The Itsy Bitsy Spider." I sang, "Toot Toot Tootsie, good bye; Toot Toot Tootsie don't cry." I shook my hands close to my ears and shuffled my feet on the hardwood floor imitating my father, who often sang at community talent shows.

I curled up beneath the keyboard and galloped my plastic horses—the bay, the pinto, and the palomino—around and between the piano legs while she played. I pretended I was Rose of Cimarron sitting at the bar with Sheriff Matt Dillon. The yeasty smell drifting from the kitchen was whiskey the cowboys drank, her shoe pumping the "loud" pedal was the horses' hooves pounding over dirt, and the swishing of her stockings was the wind sweeping down the dusty street. I was immersed in the things I loved—cowboys, horses, and my mother's music.

But when I looked up at the far-away expression on her face, my stomach knotted with worry that her music was a Pied Piper that would lure her away from us. I knew I should not speak of such things. "I can't believe a child of mine would ever worry I would abandon her," my mother would say, her eyes sad and confused. But sometimes when I felt most anxious, I reached out and lightly touched her nylon stockings to reassure myself she was solid flesh, not some spirit she'd left behind. Even then, I had to turn my face away to hide the tears that shimmered on my eyelashes.

Everything sparkles as we walk through the mist toward the Daejeon Cultural Center—pools shimmering in underwater lights; the glass foyer glittering from its perch on the hill; neon characters scaling the high-rise office building, piercing the glass of the atrium's windows and shattering into brilliant prisms; and chandeliers in the glass elevator flashing like fireflies.

The concert hall is tiered with plush seats and twinkle lights strung below steps carpeted in a fleur-de-lis pattern. Black fabric rolls in waves over the stage like thunderclouds over the prairie to announce that lightning waits in the wings to dazzle us. I study the program, looking for clues to the pieces the Daejeon Symphony will play tonight. I see the words *baielorin* and *hyeopjjugok*. I flip through my phrasebook. I think I'm reading "Mozart," "violin," "concerto," and "number five."

The soloist, in a brilliant scarlet dress, comes onto the stage. She straightens her shoulders and tucks a violin under her chin as she waits for the orchestra to begin. In the front row, a girl about three years old in velvet and lace sits on the edge of her seat, her eyes glued to the soloist.

The first movement is allegro. Its quick, staccato notes are the chittering of birds. But on the soloist's entrance, the orchestra stops while she plays an adagio, swaying back and forth as she draws a bow across the strings. She is a willow tree bending in the wind. Her dress is a camellia flower unfolding over the floor. I look at the little girl. She leans forward so far her body seems poised for flight.

Mozart's Violin Concerto Number 5 sweeps me away to a summer evening when Mozart filled the house as my father read in his chair, the breeze coming through the window lifting his thinning hair. My family owned a box set of RCA Victor Red Label records packaged in maroon boxes with names like Rachmaninoff, Beethoven, Chopin, Bach, Mozart, and Pachelbel embossed in gold on the spines. I lay on the floor next to my father's feet, listening to the music and feeling the power of music to move me from sorrow to joy. There's a tenderness I feel when I see my father's work socks sagging around his thin ankles, and I fear the fragility they expose in him.

Mother puttered in the kitchen still steamy from the hot oven and summer temperature. She wrapped pie crusts around a rolling pin, unfolded the crust into a pan, sliced green apples, and sprinkled clouds of earthy-smelling cinnamon over the fruit. "Why does he like draggy music so much? It's depressing," she griped. "Give me Elvis Presley or Bill Haley anytime."

She often said she had no appreciation for the complexities of classical music. "Your dad gets that stuff, I don't." Yet, she admired music she played for mass every week and must have known Bach, Gounod, and Handel were among those names written in gold script on those boxes.

When the orchestra reaches the finale. the musicians hold their instruments in place as the music melts into the silence. The little girl sits back in her chair looking exhausted and exhilarated. As the soloist makes her curtain call, she pops out of her seat and waves to the violinist. The woman smiles and bows to her. Walking out the hall, I glance back and see the little girl still sitting on the edge of her seat. Her mother kneels before her, coaxing her to put on her fuzzy pink coat.

Maura and I were visiting Mother at her assisted living apartment in Sioux Falls, South Dakota, only a few weeks before she died. Mother's hands lingered over piano keys until the final note faded. Then the room was hushed, except for the ticking of a grandfather clock.

Earlier, we walked to a lounge where a grand piano sat in front of a gas fireplace. The flames cast lightning over the piano's glossy black wood. "Grandma," Maura said, pulling out the bench. "Play something for me, will you please."

Mother hesitated, chewing her bottom lip. But her eyes gleamed. She sat on the bench, rubbed her knotted fingers, and began to play "Alexander's Ragtime Band."

I was heartsick at the herky-jerky melody and how her once swift and sure fingers now fumbled over the keys. I bobbed my head to the beat, forced a smile on my face. Maura clapped and cheered. "Way to boogie, Grandma." Mother laughed as she always did when people danced to her music. But when she turned to me and saw my stricken expression, her eyes darkened in knowing she played badly.

I walked to the fireplace and extended my hands toward the flames as if I were cold. But I wasn't. I didn't want my mother to see my face. I didn't want to see hers. A bowl of potpourri on the mantle smelled of roses and cinnamon, fragrances meant to cover the faint scent of the elderly. I heard the clicking of metal against hardwood as someone shuffled by with a walker. I turned back to my mother.

Sitting in front of that grand piano, she seemed as tiny as that child who had climbed up on a piano stool and stunned her family so long ago. I felt sad for my Irish grandparents, dirt farmers trying to scratch a living out of arid land. They had no money for frills like piano lessons and metronomes, and they must have grieved that loss. I wanted to weep for what might have been had Mother been born to parents of means. Would she have studied at Juilliard or Eastman School of Music? Would she have toured the grand concert halls of Europe? When I was a child I worried she would abandon me for her music. As an adult I fretted that she sacrificed her talents for me. I knew this might be my only chance to ask my mother the question I had been afraid to ask.

"Mother, do you ever wish you'd had a professional career?"

"Of course not," she said, her eyebrows furrowed. "What a ridiculous question. All I ever wanted was to have children."

There was a time I would have flinched at her words, would have seen them as a subtle but stinging criticism of my being a working mother. But by now we had negotiated the rocky terrain of expectations and disappointments in one another that once had made us stumble in our love. Now I accepted her words as truth.

Then she told a story I'd never heard before.

"I'll never forget the day your father and I moved into our first home. It was a one-room house in the middle of the prairie just west of where you grew up. Your dad had installed new linoleum on the floor. But the biggest surprise was a piano sitting in a corner. I never dreamed I would own my own piano."

When I was a little girl, I put on my mother's taffeta dress and feather cloche as if wearing her garments might help me to know who she was before she was my mother. Now I am a long-married woman who has known the small miracles of love. I see my mother throwing her arms around my father, weeping and laughing with the surprise of a piano. But even as I imagine the scene, I know it didn't happen that way. Most of my Irish family finds it difficult to express joy and sorrow except through humor. For us, laughter was the tears we couldn't shed. But Mother expressed herself through her music. So most likely Mother walked to the piano and played her gratitude for his thoughtfulness. Still, I like to imagine that she fell more deeply in love that day with a man who blessed her with such a gift.

"I wanted to play that piano all day long," Mother said.

With one finger, Mother plucked a few measures of a tune whose melody I can't now remember. Then she closed the lid over the keys, stood up, and linked her withered fingers through Maura's arm. We walked through the soft light of a quiet hallway back to her room.

CHAPTER SEVEN

I am traveling up the coastline of the East Sea on my way to the narrow spit of land that divides North and South Korea. The air is moist and redolent of salt and kelp, and the surf crashes over anti-tank barriers that spin over the beach like stars. Or maybe they are asterisks on the pages of Korean history that speak of victorious battles for inches of land but make footnotes of displaced civilians, villages reduced to rubble, and families separated by a border.

Artillery tubes peek through the branches of poplar and pine trees that blanket the hills. Watch towers with searchlights balance on stilts like egrets fishing the streams. I imagine guards—Are they North Korean or United Nation Forces?—looking through binoculars at a busload of tourists driving up Reunification Road toward the border. At several checkpoints concrete barriers protect wooden guardhouses with roofs that swoop up like winged headpieces on Polish nuns. Heavily armed South Korean soldiers walk down the aisle of our bus, inspecting our passports.

The landscape of South Dakota, too, is littered with the refuse of war—broken treaties, borders, and sorrows written in places like Wounded Knee Creek, a narrow stream that rambles through the southwest corner of the state. Greed was the cartographer that drew lines that divided the land. Cultural genocide was the truth omitted from my history books, and an old Lakota woman was once an asterisk in my diary.

I'm not certain why I make this journey. Perhaps I want to see the last vestige of the Cold War that dominated my childhood—the missile silos buried in the grasslands west of our land, bomb shelters in the basements of my school and church, and mushroom clouds that brought my mother to my bedside to wake me from nightmares. If the Cold War has ended for me, it has shadowed the lives of Koreans since 1953, when the Korean War fizzled to an inconclusive end. One hundred and sixty miles of fence and razor wire are an

71

ugly gash across the peninsula and divide families and a common people.

Maybe I am drawn by something that Jung Hun, my colleague at Chungnam National University, said. "The border makes us a melancholy people who cover our *han*, our suffering, with laughter."

Then he laughed.

Perhaps I make the journey because I know what it means to stand at the thin line between laughter and sorrow.

The bus turns off the main highway and lumbers down an isolated road. White signs hang at regular intervals on the chain link fence. "Do not come close" warn the red Hangul characters, reminders that encroaching upon the no man's land that separates North and South Korea could ignite the embers of war that still smolder beneath an uneasy truce.

They recall hand painted signs on barn wood nailed to fence posts along the gravel roads in South Dakota warning "No Trespassing." I was familiar with the word "trespassing." We said it every day in our home when I was growing up. "Forgive us our trespasses as we forgive those who trespass against us." For me sin was entangled with crossing lines, and the progression of sin was measured by lines the nun drew on the blackboard. "If you cross that first line," she cautioned, "it becomes easier to cross the next line, and the next, and then the next." She punched the lines with a piece of chalk raising shimmering swirls of chalk dust that drifted across the room. "Until finally," she said, looking over her wire-rimmed glasses, "your soul is covered in black spots of sin." I imagined pepper on mashed potatoes.

Brown birds huddle on bushes in an open meadow. They startle at the rumbling of the bus, scatter like buckshot, and fly toward North Korea. Their wings are brush strokes on a parchment of sky and bring to mind scalloped edges on boots, the leather ruffled with wear, the soles not much longer than a baby bird.

I was in high school the day Mrs. Thompson, a member of the Crow Creek tribe, stopped my mother, the boots in her hand, and said, "Please give these to Mary Alice. I wore these boots when I was a baby, and I'd like to give them to her because she's so nice to me."

The gift bothered me because I knew I hadn't earned it. I smiled and said "hello" when we passed by one another on Main Street. But I scurried past her, never stopping to talk but feeling her soft eyes following me. I didn't use the racist language some of my classmates did. We never used it in our home. So the first time I heard someone use derogatory terms for Indians, I felt a twist in my stomach, like the day I played spin the bottle in the barn with my cousins when I was a little girl.

The barn smelled of manure and the dust of oats in feed troughs. Behind me, a pinto pony nickered and pawed at straw in its stall. I don't know why I believed kissing was sinful, but I was sick at the thought of pressing my lips against a boy's. I imagined myself jumping on the pony's back, clasping his mane, and galloping away. But I wasn't brave enough to be a trick rider, nor was I brave enough to stop the game. I sat on my heels on the packed-dirt floor, my stomach churning as I watched a bottle spin, stop, and point at a boy. As I walked toward him through bars of light shining through cracks in barn wood, I was crossing a line, like the one the nun drew on the board between the sin of omission—doing nothing to stop evil—and the sin of commission—doing evil.

I lay in bed that night watching the clouds move over the stars, sick to my stomach. I crept into my parent's dark bedroom, knelt by their bed, and woke my mother. I wasn't afraid that she might spank me; she had never laid her hand on me. But I dreaded the look on her face—anger in the slight tightening of her lips, disappointment in her eyes growing dark. "Mommy," I whispered. "I did a bad thing today. I kissed a boy."

She wiped my tears with soft fingers and said, "Don't be silly. You are too young to have committed a sin. But when something makes you feel ashamed, you should not do that thing."

At first I hid Mrs. Thompson's boots on the top of my dresser, behind perfume bottles, a lacquered music box that played "Over the Rainbow," and several framed pictures of my friends. But the boots demanded my attention. So I slipped them into a drawer along with my diary and a sachet of rose petals tied in a pocket of lace. Sometimes I took them out and ran my fingers over the worn leather, hearing Mrs. Thompson's words to my mother, "Your daughter is a good girl."

But I wasn't good. Despite the queasy feeling in my stomach, I didn't confront my friends when they used racial slurs. I didn't question the stories they repeated about reservation people. I laughed at their jokes. I've learned that Buddha taught that *ipasyana* is a way of knowing through observing something so closely that the differences between the observer and the observed disappear and barriers give way. Over time, however, I began to believe the stories my friends told of how I differed from reservation people. I built a border between myself and my Indian neighbors, one stereotype and one joke at a time.

There is a poplar tree along an isolated road in the Demilitarized Zone. Someone has lopped off the top of the tree. Fire has stripped the branches of leaves and left scorch marks on the trunk. A brass plaque on a concrete base webbed with cracks sits near the tree. It marks the site where several South Korean civilians and unarmed American GIs were attacked by axe-wielding North Korean soldiers. That was August 18, 1976. Captain Arthur Boniface and First Lieutenant Mark Barrett died that day. They are among ninety other Americans who have perished in the more than thirty skirmishes that have broken out along the border since Demarcation. Now, troops on both sides of the border live in a state of readiness for war. How is it that I had never heard of these deaths? That I know so little about the Korean War and its aftermath?

The bus shudders with the engine's idling, and the smell of diesel filters through a crack in the window. I feel nauseated from the motion, the thick odor of fumes, and savage images of steel slicing through flesh. A man holds a camcorder to the window. For some reason, I am offended by his videotaping this place as if he crosses a boundary I can't define. Then a memory tugs at me. I am standing outside the Wounded Knee Cemetery waiting for the smudging ceremony to begin. A woman scans the scene with a camcorder. A native man walks over to her and puts his hand over the lens. Sacred moments must not be captured on film. She puts the camera away. Then another memory comes of a sepia-toned photo of bodies wrapped in trade blankets and stacked on the lip of a trench dug in the bloodied ground of Wounded Knee.

The carnage of Wounded Knee began in the fear of Wovoka, a prophet who taught a dance that promised the people would reclaim their land and be reunited. He said the tribes would once again follow the buffalo as they had for centuries. There were rumors that he encouraged uprisings, so when a man at a nearby agency saw the flames and smoke from Chief Spotted Elk's (Big Foot) camp, he telegraphed for military support. That was December 1890.

Although the massacre happened just a few hours west of my childhood farm, I didn't know for years that the warriors dancing and singing that night were unarmed; that there were no war songs and that a white flag flew above the council tipi; that mostly unarmed old men, women, and children—not warriors—died that day. These facts were tucked among stories of the cavalry's victorious battle in my history books as asterisks.

When I see the sign for Panmunjeom, the military complex in the heart of the Joint Security Area, my stomach knots with the edginess I once felt when I drove onto the reservation that bordered our land. My high school friends often warned me about crossing the reservation line. "Indians don't like white people, and they will beat you up if you go on the reservation," the girls said as we drove by the saloon on Main Street. They didn't talk about how later that night the police would break up fights in the alley between cowboys. "You might get killed by a drunk driver," the boys warned as we sped down gravel roads that led to river-bottom keg parties.

I wasn't always nervous about crossing the border or ill at ease with tribal people. When I was a little girl, my family sometimes watched *wacipis* in the village of Lower Brule on the river bluffs, the drums rattling the ground beneath my feet and the singers' voices echoing over the river. I wanted to join the dancers and twirl like they did, so fast that the rhinestones on my barrettes would flash like shooting stars. But I didn't dance. To join the circle of dancers uninvited seemed intrusive, like a Protestant standing at the communion railing in a Catholic church.

My father was friends with several native men, including Ted, a member of the Sicangu band, who worked for my father and lived with his wife, Rose, in a bunkhouse across the yard from us. I must have been about four years old, so my recollections may be faulty. But I see Rose chatting with my mother as the women worked in the kitchen. My father and Ted are holding pheasants in their broad hands and slicing the flesh with knives. I do remember wrapping my arms around my father's long leg, his hand ruffling my hair as he spoke a bit of Lakota with Ted. I remember the smell of mud on their boots and cigarette smoke on their jackets, the familiar scents of men and land.

Despite those good memories, I began to drive roads that bypassed the reservation.

*   *   *

At the end of the tour, I stare across the border of
Panmunjeom at a slight North Korean soldier standing in
the shadow of a building. He stares back at me, his fingers
wrapped around a rifle. His pants bag at the knees and flop
over the tops of his polished boots, and the sleeves of his
uniform reach his knuckles. He has pulled his cap so low
over his head that his ears stick out beneath the brim like
handles on a jug. He looks like a child playing soldier in his
big brother's uniform, the way I once ran through our
shelterbelt in a fringed plastic vest with a bow and arrow,
playing cowboys and Indians with my cousin. We drew straws
to decide who would play which part. Being the Indian meant
being the underdog, and even though it was just a game, I
crept behind tree trunks, fearful of being caught in the sights
of her six-shooter before I could point my arrow at her.

I recognize that feeling here in the fierce yet frightened
expression in the young soldier's eyes. I want to reach across
the border that makes us enemies, touch his smooth face,
and tell him that he has nothing to fear from me.

Borders, physical and imaginary, can both divide and
connect people, depending upon the choices we make.

In 1887, the Crooks Commission divided the Great
Sioux Lands, Oceti Sakowin, into six reservations and
opened up a pathway for travelers to follow. Miners came
through to stake claims on the veins of gold that ran through
the mountains of Paha Sapa, the Black Hills. Ranchers
staked their claims on the land. Lines drawn on paper that
day delineated not only the borders of those reservations,
but the lives of people who would live on either side of the
border in years to come.

The border that runs on the diagonal across the Korean
peninsula was drawn at the end of the war in 1953. Rear
Admiral Matthias Gardner reportedly paused only for
moments before pointing to the Thirty-eighth Parallel and
asking, "Why not put the border here?"

His impulsive decision has separated people from their
families for years.

Jung Hun's father was one of those who left North
Korea during the prisoner exchange at the end of the
Korean War. "My father walked over the Bridge of No
Return," Jung Hun tells us as we drink a beer after I lectured
on Native American literature for his class.

"My father always hoped he might one day cross back
over the bridge to his homeland," he says. "But of course he

never did. We call it the Irrevocable Bridge because we can't take back some choices."

He rubs the frosty mug with his thumb and wipes away the condensation, saying nothing for a moment. "That was last time my father ever saw his brother. Yet until the day he died, my father could recall every feature of his brother's face."

Though I can't picture Mrs. Thompson's face, I do remember her dark eyes, the flat buttons that dangled from loose threads on her coat, and her faint smell of shampoo mixed with something fried. My friends found the smell hilarious and covered their mouths to trap their giggles as we walked by her. Although my mother often smelled of Prell shampoo and fried hamburger, I put my hand over my mouth. As I followed the girls down the sidewalk, I heard my mother say, "If something makes you feel ashamed, you should not do that thing." I saw swirls of chalk dust rising between cracks in concrete.

The Military Armistice Commission building is a blue and gray Quonset hut about the size of a hen house. There is a table gleaming with polish in the middle of the room. As the Korean War raged, negotiators sat at this table, arguing over who owned more inches of land beneath it. The table still straddles the invisible border that runs beneath the floor.

A Republic of Korea soldier leads me over the border and into North Korea. He stands at the end of the table, spreads his legs, clenches his fists, and bends an elbow in a sharp angle over a glossy pistol in his holster. A young American man runs over to him and with an impish grin strikes the same pose while his girlfriend snaps pictures. The soldier stares ahead, eyes hidden behind reflective sunglasses.

An image comes to me. I am perhaps six years old and standing in front of an old Indian man sitting on a bench outside a souvenir shop in Rapid City, South Dakota. He wears a long headdress, its feathers coated in dust. His buckskin tunic is worn, the beads chipped and loose, and his leggings too short. Craters of pores cover his bulbous, old-man's nose. His knotted hands rest on his knees, their bones poking through the leather. Fingers come from somewhere behind me and tweak his nose. People laugh. I hesitate. Something feels wrong about laughing. At the same time, he doesn't seem real to me. He is simply a relic, like the arrow-heads my brothers found poking up through the pasture's sod. And so I laugh. The old man doesn't flinch. He stares ahead with cloudy eyes.

I feel hollow at the memory, and I am suddenly weary and anxious for the tour to end. I cross back over the border and lean against the wall, watching people line up to have their picture taken next to the soldier, making peace signs with their fingers. Out the window, beyond the imposing North Korean Administration Building and the armed guard standing in its shadow, a patch of blue sky rises above the scorched hills of North Korea.

It was a windy day in the fall of 1991 when I stood outside the Wounded Knee Cemetery on the Pine Ridge Reservation. All around me was the landscape of the Lakota. To the east, Mako Sika, the Badlands, with rainbow-tinged spires and gullies; to the north, Matho Paha, Bear Butte, a single hill that thrusts itself from the foothills, its summit a place for prayer and visions; to the west, Paha Sapa, the heart of the Lakota nation. To the south lies Fort Robinson, where Crazy Horse was killed.

The grasses bent sideways in the wind, their feathery tops nearly touching the ground. I imagined the pounding of hooves as the cavalry rode to forts and the squeaking of metal wheels as they cut deep grooves in the sod. To the Indians standing on this hillside, the prairie schooners must have looked like clam shells strung on a giant's necklace.

In the valley below, Chief Spotted Elk and his band of Miniconjou camped that frigid night in December. A cottonwood tree on a ridge was a lone sentry keeping watch over the long-deserted camp. I felt an immediacy of history in this place. Layered beneath the perfume of bluestem and prairie rose was the faint scent of gun powder and blood; beneath the trilling of a meadowlark, the crack of Hotchkiss guns and the screams of women and children.

I had come as a guest of the Oglala Lakota to honor the return of Zintkala Nuni, the Lost Bird, who was found lying in the snow four days after the massacre at Wounded Knee, her mother's body curled around her. I pictured a shawl wrapped around the baby, the fringes caked with her mother's blood. Perhaps there was a beaded turtle tied to the baby girl's dress, her umbilical cord inside, an amulet that protected her. Maybe she wore moccasins covered with stars of colored beads; maybe she wore leather boots.

Zintkala Nuni was adopted by an officer of the Seventh Cavalry and taken to California. Her life of poverty and abuse was a footnote to the story of the man we called a hero who took her into his home. She died on February, 14, 1920. Seventy years later, she was carried back to her homeland to lie near her mother. Her grave smelled of freshly-turned sod and carnations wrapped in a ribbon. The word "daughter" glittered on the satin.

White blocks of concrete outlined the mass grave at Wounded Knee. They sank at weary angles into the dirt as if to join the bones beneath them. Weeds pushed up through the sod and poked through the chain link fence. Like the timeless landscape of Big Foot's camp, this untended graveyard made its history more immediate somehow, as if the shooting had just stopped; this trench dug in haste, and stones tossed onto the ground to mark the site before the soldiers rode away.

That day I was nearly as old as Mrs. Thompson was when she gave me her boots, and I still wondered what she saw in that teenage girl I didn't see in myself. She must have heard my laughter, must have seen how I averted my eyes as I walked by her. I should have been no more than an aside in small print in the story of her life. But she was a woman of *wacantoognaka,* a generous heart. In the Lakota tradition of the Wopila, she gave me a gift with no expectations except perhaps her faith in the power of ceremony.

Prayer cloths tied to the fence fluttered in the wind. The pounding of drums was the heartbeat of the land, and the wind was the chants of warriors around a campfire. I closed my eyes and saw an eagle ride the thermals, carrying the people's prayers to Wakan Tanka, whose spirit resides in each of us. A man with a single braid down his back walked toward me holding a bowl of smoldering *peji hota* in his hands. I tasted the earth in the burning sage, and my eyes began to tear. I waved the smoke over me. It brushed my face with soft fingers.

CHAPTER EIGHT

A woman presses her face against a telescope's glass, moves the scope back and forth over the hills of North Korea and says, "I can see why nobody would choose to live in this desolate place."

Why does she think this place is desolate?

I stand on the balcony overlooking the DMZ at Dora Observatory, a concrete structure painted in camouflage and tucked in hills blanketed with needle-leaved shrubs and grasses. Below me, a silver ribbon of river meanders on the bias across the border, shimmering in the haze as it winds through rice fields and sloughs. It is early April, and the air is soft and smells of fertile land. This place is silent. No whine of tires or drone of engines from cars traveling the road that twists through the valley below. People speak softly, if they speak at all. Most do not. This place is so peaceful, it's easy to ignore the land mines buried along miles of barbed wire that wind through these hills, to pretend that the thousands of heavily armed soldiers who stand at the fence are ghosts of war. It's easy to forget that a country once called Keum-Su-Gang-San, the land of embroidered rivers and mountains, has been ripped down the middle by warring nations.

Earlier that day, a Republic of Korea soldier stood before floor-to-ceiling windows and spoke of battles—Pork Chop Hill, Heartbreak Ridge, the Punch Bowl. He showed slides of the hillsides behind him once pitted with bomb craters, their grasses withered by fires, and trees and shrubs stripped bare by napalm fire bombs dropped from l planes flying low over the hills. These images on the screen, more moonscape than earthly, lay in stark contrast to the thriving landscape outside the window.

Since the ceasefire in 1953, only a handful of Koreans have come back to live in the border and to farm land their families owned for generations. "With so little human interference," the soldier says, "the land has become a healthy ecosystem abundant with rivers, forests, mountains, wetlands, and prairies."

He counts on his fingers the animals, many once endangered, that now populate the DMZ—white-naped cranes, eagles, and thousands of migratory fowl, as well as Asiatic black bears, wild boars, Chinese gorals, roe deer, leopards, and lynx.

When he finishes his lecture, the soldier leads us to the balcony where telescopes are mounted on a wall. Tourists peer at the hills through the scopes, but I study the sweep of the land without the narrow perspective of a lens.

Perhaps seeing no houses, hearing no farmers tilling their fields or villagers calling to one another at street markets, the woman sees a barren space. I, on the other hand, crave the silence of South Dakota, where trapezoids and rectangles of wheat fields and prairie were a crazy quilt stitched together with dirt roads and barbwire fence lines. This patchwork of needle grass, blue stem, switchgrass, asters, wild sunflowers, and goldenrod sustained five children who roamed the prairie, a woman whose music drifted from the windows to blend with the wind, and a tall farmer who believed in the land he worked. While this former killing field has flourished, this place—so fertile in my memory—has perished.

Although I did not know it at the time, my father's death unraveled the first stitch in the tightly woven fabric of my life. I have a grainy photo of my father standing in a farmyard with three other little boys wearing overalls and newsboy caps. A sheepdog keeps watch by my father's side, his eyes alert as if looking for something to shepherd, perhaps the photographer. The boys hold a cane pole between them. Bullheads dangle from a line in a muddy strand of scales and flesh. Behind them the grasslands wear overcoats of dust that blur the seam which stitches the land to the horizon.

Lanky even as a boy, my father shoves his hands in the pockets of his wool jacket, his elbows cocked. He wears a straw hat with the brim rolled up. It perches on the back of his straw-colored hair as if challenging the wind to uproot it. He tilts his head, stares at the camera with steady eyes, and plants his boots in the sod as if he plans to stay. Did he not see the paint curling away from the boards on the corn crib? The empty hay wagon sagging into the dirt? Did that small boy not understand that such moments as this are as brief as the taste of dust on a breeze?

After my father died, my mother sold the land, a common story on the plains but singular for our family, and we scattered to braid our lives with other people in different places. For years after his death, I returned to the farm, wandering through the house and walking the cow path through the north pasture, never thinking to ask permission to return to ground now owned by a neighbor. What power did legal documents have to keep me from my place? This place once swaddled me in grass and sky and family the way Korean women wrap babies to their backs.

At the Korean Museum of Embroidery, I stop to watch a young mother bend over, balance her baby on her back, wrap a wide piece of cloth around the child, and then tie a knot beneath her breasts. The baby stares at me with dark eyes as mother and child, now twinned, stroll past framed squares of quilted fabric hanging on the walls.

We are guests of Dr. Han at this exhibit of antique *pojagi*, the quilted squares that Korean women stitched together with bits of ramie, cotton, linen, and silk. We stop to admire a piece of linen with squares and triangles of blue and green silk stitched into the cloth. Dr. Han reads the explanation of wrapping cloths hanging in a frame next to the square. "*Pojagi* express a feminine desire to weave beauty into the tedious work of tilling the fields, preserving vegetables and meat, scrubbing clothes."

Wrapping cloths, like quilts, are versatile. They can be used to cover windows, to spread over the grass at a picnic, and, most, often to carry things. Unlike leather briefcases or canvas book bags, *pojagi* conform to the shape of the objects they hold—apples from the orchard, wedding gifts or funeral food, school books, and sacred texts.

"Wrapping cloths hold memories of our lives," Dr. Han says. "I remember the wrapping scarves my mother made using clothes my grandparents and aunts and uncles wore. She said I should always think about the person who wore them. She hoped I would remember her stitching the fabric with needle and thread."

I study a framed wrapping cloth sewn with geometric shapes in a random yet harmonious pattern held together with a consistency of colors. They remind me of the quilt Ken's grandmother gave us for our wedding—squares of pink flowers, blue stripes, and rays of sun. It sheltered us in our early years and, over time, conformed to the shape of our marriage bed.

"What does *pojagi* mean," I ask Dr. Han.

"What do you call it? Um, like the mother's baby house."

"Do you mean the mother's womb?"

"Yes," he said. "Like the mother's womb, the wrapping cloths contain all possibility for life."

That piece of grassland was the *pojagi* of my childhood.

The quilt Ken's grandmother made for us now lies in a box, shredded with use, unlike our farm, which frayed over the years from neglect and misuse. The lawn threaded itself into thistle and dandelions. The shelter belt where I once lay on my stomach watching ground beetles track through cracks in the dirt is littered with dead branches from our plum trees. Chokecherries that fed sparrows are shriveled pits dangling from twigs. One summer, there was a keg party in our house, and former neighbors reported rumors of drunks tearing doors off hinges, breaking windows, and spray painting obscenities on the walls. Eventually, the owner threw gasoline on the house and set a match to it, leaving only crumbling patches of concrete now covered with creeping jenny. The rain and snow soaked the ashes into the soil and the ashes became the land itself. And in the end, not even the ashes of a life remained. I quit going back to the farm.

"My grandmother needs to see childhood land and rice fields her father harvested before she dies," I hear Gil say.

I am riding the bullet train from Seoul to Daejeon when I remember Gil's words. Off in the distance, a crane fishes in a rice field. It toils patiently, moving through the muddy water in no hurry, paying no attention to the train whizzing by. It stops, raises its head, and twists its neck, looking for minnows swimming between green stalks. Then it moves slowly forward. Its feathers above the dark water are luminous as starlight on the sea.

Gil and many of my students dream of reunification between North and South Korea so that their grandparents may once again visit the homeland they left more than sixty years ago. However, others worry a unified Korea will be a death knell to the pristine border. Dr. Pak, an environmental economist at Chungam National University, tells me that developers and industrialists on both sides of the border see the DMZ as cheap real estate. "Land within the DMZ has already been set aside for an investment zone. Plans are to build factories and plants in the border once peace is declared."

To prevent this development, international environ-mentalists have launched a campaign to register the DMZ as a transboundary preserve. "If development continues unchecked, wetlands like these," he points to a map with red lines around blue circles," will again be compromised. The white-naped crane you admire so much will lose its habitat and again be threatened by extinction."

He pauses briefly, shakes his head. "The crane is the symbol of peace for Koreans. But I fear one day it will be a victim of peace."

I check the speed of the train on a digital display board above me. One hundred and eighty-five miles an hour. But when I turn back to check on the crane, everything seems to slow down somehow. The train crawls over the tracks, the clouds mirrored in the water are still, and the bird balancing on a willowy leg is as motionless and elegant as a ballerina *en pointe*. I watch as the crane grows smaller until finally its image merges into the water.

Not long before Mother died, Ken and I drove west down Interstate 90, past fields where the air was thick with the fragrance of corn ripening, and tidy farms with painted buildings were divided yet connected by trees and corn rows into patterns of honeycombs. Come fall, tractors and combines would weave through the fields like bees through honeycomb cells.

Years after our house was scorched, the tribal biologist from the nearby Lower Brule Reservation reported seeing bald eagles raising eaglets in a cottonwood near the north dam, a pond in the pasture where my father once grazed his white-faced Herefords. Hoping to see proof of life on the deserted farmstead, we crossed the Missouri River, now buried beneath Lake Francis Case, a massive body of water created by an earthen dam upstream. When engineers opened the gates, the water flooded many Native American communities along the river bottom and displaced native people again from land they inhabited for generations. During drought years, the river level drops, and the skeletons of trees rise from the water and the shadows of houses can be seen from boats bobbing on the river. Bits of bones from old cemeteries wash up on the shore. Native people comb the muddy shoreline for the remains and rebury them on higher ground.

Just beyond the river is a stretch of gravel road that runs along the breaks, its twists and dips as familiar as the curves and hollows of my own body. This is the place where corn fields surrender to grassland and unkempt spaces.

Machinery rusts near the ditches. Cattle graze in the shadows of sagging buildings. The gaps between the boards of abandoned houses are windows into the lives of those who came here and to the failed dreams that pushed them farther west. But land is a tenacious thing. In the way that native tribes bury the baby's umbilical cord to root that child forever to the land, this landscape buries itself in the soul. Most of us who have long ago moved away from here have never really left.

At Sunny Slope Farm, home to our nearest neighbors, the road turned north and then angled west again. Our car bounced over the washboard ridges of the dirt road that led to our farmyard. We passed the black-and-yellow Chevy I drove away to attend the university. It has made a home in the weeds, and sparrows have tucked their nests into the crevices of the windshield.

Weathered-gray boards are scattered like bones after battle in the feedlot, and we walked through buffalo grass past the granary. The granary roof was my refuge when I was small. I lay on the slant, studying the clouds, the wooden shingles scratching my bare legs. The smell of mud mingled with the yeasty fragrance of wheat warmed by summer heat in the bins below me. The wind muffled sound and wrapped me in silence, except for the drone of my father's tractor circling the field. On rare days, an airplane passed overhead, and as I watched the contrails fade, I dreamed of traveling to foreign lands, secure in knowing that this place would be waiting for my return.

Ken and I crawled over the gate and hiked the cattle path toward the pond. There was the smell of dust, not the dusty smell mixed with cattle hide and manure that once permeated this pasture, but the smell of something dry and withered. Scattered along the path were the bleached bones of mice and birds. Even as a child I knew that I shared the prairie with predators, including rattlesnakes that might be coiled along the path. So I walked in stops and starts, listening for the shushing warning sound of a snake ready to strike. This pasture taught me that beauty and danger are often woven into a single cloth.

Tractor tires cut deep ruts in the track, but I felt the old trail beneath my feet guiding me to the pond. Abruptly, it disappeared into rows of towering sorghum. Their dry leaves rustled in the wind. I stopped and looked east for that hollow in the dirt where I was told buffalo once wallowed. I looked north for the expanse of horizon that had always guided me. I couldn't see anything but stalks of sorghum. Disoriented and frightened, I called, "Ken. This isn't the north pasture. I don't know where I am."

Then I realized the sorghum field blocked my view. When had this prairie been plowed? Why hadn't someone told me? Without that seam of grass and sky to guide me, I was lost and untethered.

For the first time in my life, I felt as if I were trespassing on my own land.

When we reached the dam, I pushed my way through thick grasses and chokecherry bushes. I heard my mother's voice. *Don't go down to the pond by yourself. If you drown, it will be days before we find your body.* But having warned me, she generally stayed in the house while I sneaked down to the dam to wade in the waters capturing minnows and garter snakes. If she knew I disobeyed, she didn't let on. Maybe she felt she did her duty by warning me. Maybe she assumed older siblings would watch out for me. When I became a mother, I understood she probably craved silence.

But on inexplicable days, Mother drove us to the dam, despite being unable to swim and terrified of water. She sat in the car and honked the horn whenever we ventured too far from shore. Beneath the wind blowing through the grass I heard "You kids get back here right now." Most often, we turned around at the first blare, but sometimes we dog paddled away from the dam's bank as the honking became a mournful wail, as my mother watched her children swim away from her.

Lyman County was suffering a drought that year, and the pond's waters had retreated. Cracks like spider webs radiated over the shoreline. Once, red-winged blackbirds swayed on cigars of velveteen cattails that lined the pond. Badgers scuttled toward the bank, leaving ripples through the tall grass, and dragonflies were helicopters skimming the water, their cellophane wings glittering. Had drought forced them to migrate? Or had they fled like refugees when the combines and tractors rumbled into this pasture?

I knelt to wedge my thumb in a crack and watched the soil crumble. A gust of wind picked up the loose sod, and it swirled into the air. I leaned over the pond, cupped my hands, dipped them in the water, and brought my hands to my face. The water was rank and lifeless.

To the west, Medicine Butte, the reliable compass point in my life, led me in the direction of a cottonwood at the end of the dam. At the bottom of its trunk lay a pile of bones, feathers, and fish skeletons. Tucked in the highest branches of the tree was a hubcap-sized nest woven of thick twigs. We waited under the cottonwood, hoping to hear the stuttering chirping of an eagle. A crack of a pistol shattered the silence, the sound plows made when they first broke the roots. But it was only an engine backfiring.

If it is true that everything in the universe contains in itself the universe, did the trees in Asia hear the snapping of these roots? Did their own roots shudder? When bombs scarred the Korean hills and napalm stripped the leaves from the shrubs that spread across them, did the grasslands wither and die? Did the tendrils of grass feel their grip on the land loosening?

We walked back to the car in the hush of mourners.

On the way home, we stopped to visit my mother at her apartment in an assisted living facility. When I told her the pasture had been plowed, she wept. "Your father would never have turned over that piece of land. That was his favorite pasture."

Who knows if my father would have left this patch of prairie untouched? Like the neighbor who now owns this land, he had taxes to pay, expenses for seed and fertilizer, and veterinarian bills. And my father was ambitious and focused on securing a better future for his children. If he were alive today, would he, too, plow over old sod to plant corn or sorghum and profit from record prices? Maybe—I don't know. But in over thirty years of farming, he only broke eighty acres in a corner of this pasture. He planted a field of milo there, and when he had time, he drove out to the field to watch the prairie grouse dart between the rows of maroon-colored plumes and to listen to their mating calls.

I believed that my mother feared the land and huddled inside our house, her safe island in a sea of hostile prairie. As a child, I felt constrained by my mother's fears. As a mother, I understand them. The land threatened us as much as it sustained us. But now I wonder if perhaps my mother loved and understood this place as much as my father did, but in different ways. When I rode on the tailgate of our old pickup as it bounced over the hollowed-out places of the pasture, I could hear my father counting the number of calves sucking at their mother's teats, noting their alert bodies. My mother spotted a white patch behind the ear of a bull calf. When my father saw the grain fields ripening, she spied a pink prairie rose creeping along the fence line.

Perhaps my mother's sorrow at the plowing of the north pasture was *han*, a grief so primal it predates words, a sadness that can be neither defined nor explained. It's possible that she did not have the strength to own such pain, and so she assigned it to my father. Or perhaps, after long years of living through loss after loss after loss, she saw the turning over of ancient sod and the ripping of the root system that once knit the land together as one final tear in the tattered edges of her life.

CHAPTER NINE

I sit on a stone bench near a lotus pond, sipping *nokcha*—tea made from tender leaves grown on the rolling hills near Boseong on the southern tip of Korea. Steam rising from the cup warms my face. There is the taste of soil. Although snow still sparkles on the mountains, the late February sun is bright, and shoots of green poking through the sod hint of spring. A lotus pond is a place meant for reflection and tranquility. But today, it is a place for panic. One week before classes begin, I have learned that instead of American Literature, I will be teaching English Conversation, a course for which I have no training or experience.

After a week of being unnerved by the city with its unfamiliar sounds and smells, of adjusting to our meager housing, I was eager to get into the classroom where I feel at home. Now, I think of the poems by Robert Frost, Jane Kenyon, William Stafford, Emily Dickenson, and Walt Whitman I carried with me on the airplane and the lecture notes and assignments now useless as well. My thirty-five years of teaching experience fold back to 1969 when I was a novice standing outside the classroom, terrified at the thought of teaching high school seniors. Now it's teaching students at Chungnam National University that worries me.

The CNU campus begins in a valley and spreads over the foothills of the Charyeong Mountain range. Many of the buildings are concrete block with small windows, hastily-constructed and utilitarian Cold War structures. Universities like this one were conceived in the tragedy of a bloody civil war and born in the conviction that an educated citizenry would assure Korea would never be defeated again. Inspired by the old proverb "When the house is burnt, pick up the nails," South Koreans dug through the rubble of war and, with sprinter's speed, rebuilt their country, earning the nickname "The Miracle on the River Han." Chungnam National University was built with funds raised by citizens who sold property, cattle, and crops to raise money for the construction of the first buildings.

In a break from centuries of Confucian convention that excluded most females from formal education, Korean girls began to attend universities after the Korean War. My father, too, was determined to see his daughters earn college degrees, and like the Koreans, he funded our education through the sale of livestock and crops. He valued learning for its own sake. "An education is the one thing nobody can take from you," he often said. But he also believed in the practicality of furthering our learning. "You need a profession to fall back on should something happen to your husband." That conversation occurred in the early sixties. Like most men at that time, he probably did not anticipate his daughters would pursue careers.

My sister, Jeanne, was among the first generation of women expected to earn college degrees but never use them. Mine was the generation expected to earn a degree and work, but only in fields considered appropriate for women—secretaries, nurses, teachers, and for Catholic girls like me, nuns. By the time I was in high school, I knew I wouldn't "take the veil." I resisted a career in education because I thought all teachers were like Miss Brooks on the popular television show, prim women with curled-under bangs and pencils behind their ears who wore sensible shoes and blouses with Peter Pan collars, women who were too dowdy to attract a man and so doomed to renting rooms in married-women's houses.

In high school, I aspired to be Brenda Starr. I had worked on the school newspaper and could crank out a story quickly because the writing was formulaic and I was a speedy typist. Journalism was the only writing I could imagine doing. I had never met someone who had actually published a book. Authors didn't live in the flyover country of South Dakota, especially women writers, except for Laura Ingalls Wilder, who had the advantage of being a pioneer girl. Real writers were those I studied in high school— Charles Dickens, Edgar Allan Poe, John Keats, William Wordsworth, William Shakespeare, and Steven Crane. Leading a writer's life was a pipe dream for girls like me who scribbled stories in notebooks and hid them in the back of their closets.

Goldfish glide through the tangle of brown lotus roots, their scales flashes of light in the pond's murky water. I imagine the roots digging into the mud, spinning cells and fibers into buds that will blossom, the way my father spun words into stories. My father was the first to teach me the magic of stories, tucking my siblings and me into bed and inventing tales, my favorite being one about airplane rides to the North Pole. He blew air between his lips—*pupp, pupp, pupp*—as the plane taxied down the runway. His forearms strained when he pulled back on the yoke, and the engine groaned—*grrrr*—with the plane's acceleration. Although I had never flown before, I knew how it would feel to ride in an open cockpit, to see the sun glinting off the wing, and feel my hair flying behind me as I was lifted into the sky.

I took a poetry class with Kathleen Nagle in the fall of 1966, my sophomore year at South Dakota State University. She was a tiny woman with snowy hair pulled back in a bun and anchored with a black bow. Her eyes were the blue of Siamese cats and her Irish-pale cheeks rosy as if she were always coming in from the cold. She wore pearl earrings and hand painted, floral scarves draped over turtleneck sweaters. They gave a touch of opulence to the classroom in Engineering Hall where the desktops were often covered with penciled calculations and faint clouds of chalk dust hung in the air. One November day she read from T. S. Eliot, her voice caressing the words. "I grow old, I grow old. I shall wear the bottoms of my trousers rolled." I was miles from the sea, yet I walked the beach with J. Alfred Prufrock and felt the sand tugging at my toes as the tide pulled the grains back to the sea. At Thanksgiving I told my parents I was changing my major from journalism to English.

I took creative writing from Mrs. Nagle the next semester. We met in a library room warmed by the morning sun. I sipped coffee with cream and nibbled on cake donuts. Outside the window, I could see the campanile towering over students who scurried across the campus green. The chimes striking the hour warned that they were late for class. There was the smell of old paper and ink in the books stacked below. Beneath Mrs. Nagle's voice reading our work was the clanging of steps as librarians ran down to the basement to gather materials for faculty and students. She gave the same respect for our words as she had for T.S. Eliot's, pausing to let phrases grab us with their inventiveness or elegance. I felt terror and exhilaration as she read my poems and stories. I peeked from beneath my bangs at the other students, gauging what they thought of my writing.

The poet Gwendolyn Brooks came to campus for a poetry reading that semester. She was tall with elegant hands, hair tucked under a multi-colored scarf, and a deep, melodic voice. This was the first time I had ever heard a writer read.

"We, real cool/ We, left school/ We, lurk late/We,. . ."

I didn't know poetry could sound like that—syllables rising and falling, pauses held forever, line breaks syncopated as jazz. Poems opened up for me that year in the way that flowers unfold their petals layer by layer.

Somehow Mrs. Nagle had convinced Ms. Brooks to read our short stories. If this amazing woman liked my story, I thought, maybe I could be a writer. But her praise had to be glowing. Anything less would prove what I already suspected—girls like me didn't become authors. She read my story "Wasted Dresses and Winter Decisions," an overwrought telling of a senior in high school who breaks up with her boyfriend even though he is kind and their relationship is comfortable. But she plans to attend college, and he will keep his job at a gas station. One night, she tries on her dress for the winter formal, looks in the mirror, and sees a girl who can't live the life he imagines for them. She folds the dress into a plastic bag and puts it in the bottom drawer of her dresser.

Mrs. Nagle returned our stories with the poet's handwritten critique stapled to the corner. I didn't open the note in class because I didn't want the other students to see my reaction to what I expected would be a negative response. When I got back to my room, I held the note for several minutes, my stomach churning. Finally I tugged at the staples and quickly scanned what she said about the alliteration in my title and the narrative's honesty. Between her brief and not unkind words, I read, "You're not good at this." I crumpled the note and threw it in the wastebasket. The next morning, I hiked across the campus to the education department and enrolled in education.

When I graduated college in June of 1968, English education majors were flooding high schools with applications for positions that didn't exist. In my only interview that spring, I shifted nervously in the chair, the snaps on my garter belt digging into my thighs, my hands sweaty. "Well, I hate to tell you this," the principal said, "but English teachers are a dime a dozen."

I remembered my father's words. "If you want to study literature, go into education. We will always need good English teachers." I left the interview ready to do battle with my father for placing faith in a useless education degree. We never had that argument. Shortly after the interview, he was diagnosed with cancer and died three months later. His conviction that a teaching degree would guarantee me a job seemed no more naïve than my childish certainty that my life would always be secure.

In August, Ken and I moved to Aberdeen, where he enrolled at Northern State University. I found a job as a society page writer at the *Aberdeen American News*. I collected recipes from the wire services and wrote feature stories about local cooks, but mostly I retyped engagement notices and accounts of weddings, and, when the city reporter was busy, obituaries. I never once chased a story the way Brenda did, pencil and notebook in hand and a press pass bouncing on a string around my neck. Still there were perks. I could smoke at my desk while I typed stories and hang out in the press room with its smell of ink and Lava soap on the hands of men arranging letters into wooden trays. I could hear the rumble of the linotype and the chatter of news unfolding on ticker tape from the AP teleprinter. Sometimes I held the strip of paper in my hands thinking of people all over the world bent over typewriters generating words.

In January of 1969, I was hired to teach senior English at Aberdeen Central High School, replacing a woman forced to resign because she was pregnant in violation of her contract. My class room was in an old building at the opposite end of the block from the other English teachers. The Home Economics department was across the hall. The teacher was a thin woman rigid with rules. She seldom spoke to me, but narrowed her eyes as she shut her classroom door when my students were rowdy, as they often were. I came from a rural high school populated with compliant kids. We accepted rules we didn't like and teachers we didn't respect. Central was crammed with nearly twelve hundred students. They listened to Jimi Hendrix and Janice Joplin, smoked in the bathrooms, whispered of drug use, and tossed pencils at one another or slept during my lectures on Beowulf and Chaucer. "What does this have to do with real life?" they asked of the stories we read. I couldn't answer their question.

After several years of teaching high school, I applied for graduate school at SDSU. I called Mrs. Nagle for a recommendation, and she invited me to her home to discuss my application. She was in her late sixties by then, retired, and living in a cottage not far from campus. She still wore pearl earrings and hand painted scarves, but her fair skin was wrinkled and her spine had settled deeply into her hips making her even shorter than she was when I first met her. She served shortbread cookies and tea with lemon in china cups with pink roses. We chatted about my brief journalism career and high school teaching experiences. Finally, she asked why I wanted to enter graduate school. I remembered how often I looked out the classroom window, knowing I was ill-prepared to teach literature to high school students. "I want to learn more about my discipline," I said. "I didn't know what I needed to know about English until I tried to teach it."

She studied me, her blue eyes still clear. "You know, I've always regretted not encouraging you to keep writing. I thought your work showed promise." I was certain she was just being kind.

I leave the lotus pond now and walk up the hill to our apartment to meet Sunnhee Kim, a first year English teacher at an elementary school. We met her a day after we arrived in Korea. Dr. Nho asked Ken to be her conversation buddy as we sipped *makgeolli*, milky rice wine, after a meal of mudfish soup—chunks of an eel-like fish served in a thin broth and sprinkled with slivers of green onions and bits of garlic. "She's very nervous about speaking English and wants to practice with an American."

She enters our apartment, a tiny woman dressed in a jacket covered in pink flowers, and a blue ribbon in her hair. She slips off her sandals, glides over the floor in white anklets, kneels, and tucks her skirt around her knees. She looks up at Ken, her eyes shining. "Mr. Ken, I have dreamed of being English teacher since I was little girl. I'm so grateful you help with my dream." She covers her mouth and giggles.

Her youthful demeanor disguises her determination to improve her English. She listens to Voice of America radio every night until midnight and wakes up at five AM to read magazine articles online and participate in an English-speaking chat room. "I want to achieve a perfect score on the English Proficiency Exam and teach for five years," she says. She lifts a tea bag from her cup, wraps it around a spoon, and squeezes the bag as carefully as she chooses her words. "Then I will earn my doctorate and become an administrator of an elementary school." It's hard to imagine anything stopping this young woman from reaching her goals.

Ken tells her we would like to visit her class one day. She claps her hands. "I will please the school president if I bring a foreigner to school. And I will be very popular with the students because most have never met a foreigner."

The next week, on a chilly day in early March, Miss Kim meets us at the school's front entrance and hands us a pair of rubber slippers. We slide our feet into them, clench our toes to keep them on our feet, and shuffle down the hall. Children stop, cover their mouths, and stare. One little guy drops to his knees and kowtows. When we walk into the classroom, there is a gasp, silence, and then the clattering of desks sliding across the floor as children leap from their chairs, cheering and clapping.

We talk about fifth graders in America. What books and movies they like and what they like to eat. Our stories of South Dakota inspire one boy who lived in Michigan where his father earned his PhD to tell tales about his visit to our state. "In the Reptile Gardens, I held snake this big"— he stretches his arms wide and the children gasp—"and saw buffalo stampeding in Custer Park."

Perhaps, he embellishes the length of the snake and the stampeding buffalo, but he tells his tale with the breath- less conviction of all good storytellers, and the other children listen with astonished eyes. Miss Kim stands in the corner twisting her skirt with her tiny hands and chewing on her lip. When he is done, she does not praise him for his fluent English, but rather begins a whole-class recitation.

"What do American children like to eat?"

"Pizza!"

"What books do American children read?"

"Harry Potter!"

At the end of class she tells her students, "All your dreams will come true if you shake the hand of a Westerner." The children leap from their desks and rush to the front of the room, pushing us against the blackboard as they reach for our hands. I now understand why so many Korean children run up to us shouting, "I like pizza. I love America." They think we are wizards of a magic language.

We call Miss Kim a year or so after leaving Korea. When I ask how she did on the English exam, there is a pause. "It was ok," she says.

"Are you working on your doctorate?"

Another pause. "No. I met a man at a church conference. I think we'll be married and start a family right away. I won't have time to go to school then."

She confesses that students who have lived in the United States speak better English than she does. "I was bad teacher because my students know more than I do."

I tell her how I struggled my first year of teaching and how on a particularly bad day, I put my head on my desk and sobbed, certain I would lose my job. "When I didn't lose my position," I say, "I went from classroom to classroom seeking the advice of experienced teachers. I spent the summer planning lessons and reading new books. Miss Kim, I learned how to teach and so can you."

"Korean government spends a lot of money on English programs," she says. Her voice sounds very far away and I strain to hear her. "I shamed myself and I let my country down because I couldn't learn better English. I need to go." There was a click, and the line went dead. The next time we tried to call her, the number, or perhaps her last name, had been changed.

The day after our visit to Miss Kim's school, I walk under the branches of cherry trees laden with tight buds. I am on my way to my first English Conversation class, armed with a briefcase of lecture notes and assignments. My brain is still reeling with advice from Linda, a Scottish woman with auburn hair and freckles who also teaches English here.

I met her the day I learned of my change in teaching assignment. I knocked on her door in the International Studies building, a new and glitzy structure of marble and glass that houses the Foreign Language Institute. "Can you help me, please? I just found out I'm teaching English as a second language. I'm in over my head."

She invited me into her office cluttered with books, stacks of paper, and figurines of Buddha. A poem from the quatrains of Kuan Yin hung on the wall behind her. "Pause here and breathe/ take time to drink your tea." She did, in fact, offer me a cup of tea, which we sipped as I asked questions about teaching English as a Foreign Language. She pulled files from a metal cabinet and searched the computer for websites for ESL teachers. Eventually we cobbled together my English conversation class.

"You know," she said, "few of your students will be proficient in English. Most have never met a foreigner, so they will be excited, but nervous about taking a class from you, more nervous than you are now."

A week later, I wander through a sculpture garden among stone lanterns, pagodas, and lotus flowers. In an open area, barefooted men and women in white tunics and loose trousers lift their legs and bend their arms in angles. I watch them for several minutes. They move with the serenity of cranes gliding through the water. The birds seem always to be at home wherever they are—in marshes and rice fields, lotus ponds and streams.

The afternoon I read Ms. Brook's critique of my story, I struggled to know where I belonged. I put a Nancy Wilson record on the turntable and sat on my bed smoking cigarettes until my eyes burned and my lungs felt heavy. There was a tobacco leaf stuck to my tongue. I picked it off and rubbed it between my fingers. It left a faint stain. I thought of Mrs. Smith, my high school English teacher. She was kind and committed to teaching her students to love literature. But in my memory her fingers were often blotchy with red ink and her blouse smelled of chalk dust. She taught in a dusty classroom, stacks of ungraded papers and tests on her desk. If being an author was glamorous, being a teacher was tedious. If writers were famous, teachers were anonymous. For over an hour, the arm on the record player lifted, settled the needle into the grove, and rode the ridges to the center of the record before starting all over again. I felt stuck in a pattern as well—education classes and then years of teaching.

A friend had given me a copy of *Up the Down Staircase,* by Bel Kaufman, the story of Sylvia Barrett, a young English teacher in an inner city school in New York City. Her students wrote notes to her that spoke of hope and despair, unhappiness and joy, poverty and racism, and the longing for love. Miss Barrett told them, "If you deny what you know, or what you are, or where you are, you deny the simplest part of being alive." I read in the narrow circle of light cast by the reading lamp feeling something stir in me. If I couldn't be a writer, then perhaps, like Miss Barrett, I could offer young people the solace of expressing themselves and, like Mrs. Nagle, introduce them to literature that would help them make sense of their lives.

I leave the sculpture garden and hike down the hill toward the English department where my Korean students wait for me. By April the branches on the canopy of cherry trees above me will be so heavy with white and pink blossoms they will touch the sidewalks. The city will string twinkle lights on the trees, and hundreds of people will come to campus for the Cherry Blossom Festival where the streets are lined with food booths and musicians in traditional clothing play ancient instruments in the square. Children will stand under the glittering branches while their parents snap their pictures. One little boy will run up to us yelling, "It fairy land! It fairy land!" He will be right. By April, I will walk to class through a shower of petals, eager to be in the classroom once again.

"He plants his boots in the sod as if he plans to stay." (My father — standing next to the dog, an unidentified neighbor boy, Uncle Frank, and Uncle George, Lyman County around 1917.)

". . . her eyes hint at the determination that will sustain her." (Mother holding me, in front of my Grandmother McManus' house, photo taken in 1947.)

". . . land is a tenacious thing. . . it buries itself in the soul." (Our deserted farmstead in Lyman County.)

"a child. . . can sense the harmony in the way that sensuousness and spirituality are entwined." (Tongil Daebul, Seoraksan National Park.)

". . . the child looking at the woman her daughter will become." (Mother on her tricycle, taken around 1921.)

". . . this woman who weaves symbols of maternal love. . . into knots." (Yoong Seung Yi at her *maedeup* shop in Gung Dong.)

" . . . negotiators sat this table arguing over who owned more inches of land beneath it." (Republic of Korea soldier stands at the end of the negotiation table at Panmunjeom.)

" . . . nobody went to weddings in those days." (My parents on their wedding day. From left to right: Frank Woster, Henry Woster, Marie McManus Woster, Dolores McManus.)

". . . in Hahoe, the past. . . collides with the present." (Satellite dish on mud and brick house in Hahoe.)

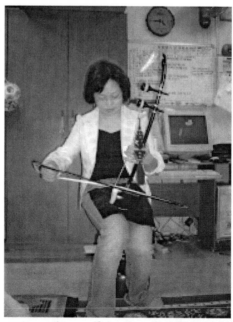

". . . the song expresses the soulful nature that Irish and Koreans share." ("Danny Boy" played at Korean Traditional Music Museum.)

". . . if everything contains in itself. . . the universe, did the trees in Asia hear the snapping of roots?" (The pond in the north pasture.)

CHAPTER TEN

On Easter Saturday afternoon, we walk among students, cell phones to their ears, as they amble down the sidewalk on their way to the pubs and boutiques in Gung Dong. Buses rumble past farmers sitting on the sidewalk selling vegetables. Diesel fumes mingle with the tangy aroma of Korean barbeque from food carts. I can almost taste the spicy pork wrapped in crisp lettuce leaves. At the intersection of two busy streets, we wander into the foyer of a Catholic church where a man wrestles a Pascal candle into a brass stand. He stops his task and walks toward us, smiling, a dignified man in a herringbone sports coat and khaki pants, his silver hair swept up in a pompadour. "Hello, my name is Thomas Aquinas."

Thomas Aquinas? Is this man a bit off-kilter? Is he a priest who changed his name at ordination? Ken offers his hand to him. "I'm Ken, and this is my wife, Mary." Thomas Aquinas wraps his fingers around mine. They are warm and dry despite the damp chill in this glass and concrete foyer. I try to look as if I'm accustomed to meeting the ghosts of theologians. But I don't fool him.

"I see you're puzzled by my name," he says. "Many Koreans choose English names along with their Korean names. I chose Thomas Aquinas because I admire his writing. His words inspired me to become a Catholic deacon."

"Are you Catholic or Christian, Miss Mary?" he asks.

I would phrase the question differently. Do I have a spiritual home, and if so, where? Although I have not attended mass for some time, I will always feel Catholic because of my childhood church in Reliance. St. Mary's perched on a knoll at the intersection of two gravel streets. Juniper bushes stood guard at the front door like *janseung*, the intricately carved totem poles that once kept watch at the entrances of Korean villages. Steps creaked as I followed my parents to the choir loft, past a window with pastel squares of glass and a sill bleached by the sun. A pump organ stood under the window, its keys yellowed with age and

105

hollowed from the friction of fingers. White knobs stamped with words like *bass forte* and *voix celeste* ran in a row above the keys. The squiggles on the knobs spoke a language I didn't know but understood in the change of vibrato and tone when my mother pushed them in and out. Sometimes I curled up on the floor near the organ and fell asleep to her nylon stockings whispering like siblings in their beds as she pumped the pedals up and down.

I was nourished by images of family in the chapel. Mary robed in blue and white, the baby with stars glittering over his head, and the sandal-footed Joseph in brown garment and rope tied around his waist. My little brother and cousins slept on benches, arms and legs splayed, while older kids made faces at one another behind our hands. Aunts and uncles bent over the pews, rosaries woven through their fingers.

The Catholic mass was my first experience with classical music—Bach, Beethoven, Handel. Latin and Gregorian Chants were lessons in poetry. The chapel was infused with sensuousness—light and shadow, sound and silence, marble and linen, pale and vivid colors. Although I didn't have words to express it, those senses merged in ways that offered a sense of harmony and security. Perhaps I'll never again feel at home the way I did in that church.

Thomas Aquinas interrupts my thoughts. "Would you like a tour?"

"Of course, I would love one," I say, having no idea how much this urban church in Korea with its abstract designs, its lack of gilding, color, and realistic images, would unsettle me and yet spark comforting memories of that church in Reliance. We walk past a massive baptismal font carved from black granite. Sheets of water run down the sides and pool in a shallow basin. I put my hand under the stream remembering the feeling of running my fingers through a slick coating on the bottom of a white font shaped like a lily that stood just inside St. Mary's chapel. My father knelt before me, his hand warm as he guided my fingers from forehead, chest, and shoulders while we prayed, "In the name of the Father, and of the Son, and of the Holy Ghost."

Thomas Aquinas leads us outside to a courtyard where hyacinth and lilies curve in a half moon around a limestone statue of the Blessed Virgin. At her feet, a glass votive holds an unlighted candle. Her face and robe are carved in sharp lines. Her hands are shapeless against her flat chest, and her eyes are discs that look at me with indifference. She is nothing like Mary in my childhood church whose blue robe draped over her womanly breasts, whose eyes were warmed by the candlelight, her skin luminous in the glow. She extended her hands toward me, and I longed to wrap my arms around the folds of her robe, lean into her hip, and feel her fingers in my hair.

"Architects designed the building to resemble Noah's Ark." Thomas Aquinas points to a statue of Christ hovering on a soot-stippled ribbon of steel wrapped around the second story of the church. "The ledge is the ship's hull and the statue of Christ its figurehead."

Behind the statue, a red neon cross soars from the church's roof into the smog. I recall the night we arrived in Korea. As we drove away from the airport, I stared out the window of our conveyance van at hundreds of red crosses glowing above the Seoul high rises like a celestial cemetery. Why did Korea need so many Red Cross offices, I wondered. Were disasters that common in this country? I imagined cities leveled by hurricanes and earthquakes. Home seemed very far away that night.

"Is there a Red Cross office here?" I ask Thomas Aquinas.

"No, a red cross signifies a church. There are more than fifty thousand Christian churches in Korea, but we have little land for construction of new buildings. So congregations share a building, and each erects its own cross."

The Korean crosses jarred memories of another cross rising from the peaked roof of St. Mary's and merging seamlessly with the sky. In summer, the cross glimmered in the heat waves rising from the tarpaper shingles; in winter, it vanished into the gray clouds. On dark nights, as we drove to Friday rosary services, I curled up on my mother's lap knowing without proof that the cross still hung in the heavens and guided my family to our spiritual home.

Thomas Aquinas says, "I'll show you the sanctuary now." We walk up the steps (because of space shortage many sanctuaries in Korea are housed on the second floor) into a room with dun-colored walls, woodwork, and bricks. The sun shining through rose-colored waves in the windows casts a coral sunset over the altar and somehow softens the chapel and the figure of Christ hanging on the back wall. Thomas Aquinas points to arched beams spanning the ceiling. "Those beams are the keels, or the core that supports a ship the way Rome sustains the faithful. This chapel symbolizes a stable vessel in a turbulent sea." He turns in a circle, sweeps his arm around the room, and draws me into the metaphor of ships and safe harbors.

I recall a misty day in Ireland when Ken and I came upon a crumbling stone church in a hillside village. We wandered to the back and found a kelly green container as large as a propane tank. On the front were the words "Holy Water." At the bottom was a metal spigot. We joked that in Ireland even holy water came in casks. But as we drove down the twisting road to the next village, I couldn't help feeling as if a curtain had been drawn to reveal a little man spinning knobs and dials. I envy the certainty of Thomas Aquinas' faith.

Thomas Aquinas asks again, "Are you Catholic or Christian?

My stomach tightens as it did in high school when Protestant friends accused me of belonging to a superstitious church. "Why do you make that distinction?" I ask.

"There are so many different Protestant churches," he says. "Methodist, Baptist, Lutheran. It's easier just to call them Christian. There's only one Catholic Church."

If his question was innocent, I suspected my friends had darker motives. "You kneel before statues," some said. "That's idolatry." I didn't tell them I found their sanctuaries cold and unfriendly, their services dull and pragmatic. "You worship Mary," others accused, pointing to my sterling silver medal of the Virgin around my neck. I couldn't explain the intimacy I felt with Mary when I traced the blue glaze of her robe with my finger. As a teenager, I responded by flaunting my faith the way I wore the sooty cross Father imprinted on my forehead on Ash Wednesdays. I blessed myself when I drove with my girlfriends past the church, and I smacked my Friday tuna fish casserole in the school lunch room with self-righteous satisfaction while my Protestant friends picked at the spongy noodles.

Thomas Aquinas waits for my answer. How can I tell this faith-filled man I am no longer at home in the Catholic Church? I take the coward's way out. "We are Catholic." He runs into an office and brings back a sheet of paper on which he has written the times for services. "Please join us tomorrow for mass."

On Easter Sunday, Thomas Aquinas ushers us into the sanctuary, where the fragrance of lilies and moss is layered with the scent of incense smoldering in a brass *thurible*. He prods people to scoot over. The pew creaks with their weight as they slide across the wood. I remember a creaking sound in St. Mary's as my aunts and uncles shifted on the kneelers. They were accustomed to kneeling—pulling a calf coming breech or tightening the lug nut on a tractor tire, scrubbing floors, and pulling potatoes. They believed in Christ's example of patient suffering. They didn't have time or inclination to question their faith.

Women around me bow their heads, their glossy black hair shining through mantillas. A few women in designer suits wear nothing on their perfectly-coiffed hair. Some women cover their hair with a hanky or Kleenex. Mother often pulled a bobby pin out of her purse, opened it with her teeth, and fastened her embroidered handkerchief to my hair, the smell of spit and linen vivid in my imagination. One Sunday when I was in high school, I declared, "I'm done wearing a hanky on my head." She sighed, put the hankie away, and said, "You're just trying to be a modern Catholic."

"Modern" described most things that weren't what she considered "old fashioned" and so suspicious.

The quivering note of a *haegeum* rises above the rumble of traffic coming through the windows. Soon more strings play Pachelbel's Canon with a patient loveliness. When the prelude is finished, the priest processes down the aisle as the choir sings "Christ the Lord is Risen Today." Their voices are clear, their harmonies sure. Electronic keyboards, violins, as well *ajaeng*, *haegeum*, *piri*, and *janggos* accompany them. Throughout the liturgy, a choir and chamber orchestra blend Latin hymns and Korean folk songs into music that is tribal and joyous.

I remember years ago my mother explaining to me how the arrangement of notes on staffs created music, the way words on paper made poetry. "Sometimes, when you read a poem," she said, "you come across a phrase so striking that you realize no other combination of words could create that image. That's how it is when I hear a pure chord like the one your dad and Uncle Bill sang in *Panis Angelicus*. No other possible arrangement of notes could make such a perfect sound." She paused and cocked her head as if she were hearing once again that musical shift so subtle it might have been missed. That moment when my father came in on the offbeat to hold a perfect harmonic note under Uncle Bill's melody. "So perfect," she said. "You feel a chill."

At the chancel, Father genuflects and looks to the crucifix as he blesses himself. "*In nomine Patris et Filli, et Spiritus Sancti. Amen.*" Then, to remind us of our salvation through baptism, he marches down the aisle with a silver bucket in one hand, an *aspergillum* in the other. He dips the *aspergillum* in the bucket, raises it over his head, and gives a shake that sends an arc of water across the church and dampens my face. The woman next to me wipes her face with her hankie, but I let the water evaporate on my skin as I always do. Growing up in a place where heat wrinkles the soil and the air is so dry it seems to crackle, cool water against my face is the gift of baptism.

I am surprised by the laughter and even applause when the priest gives his homily. But their laughter offers a feeling of community as warm as the sunlight filtering through stained glass. Unable to understand the Hangul, I am a child again at a time when Latin was the joy of rhythm and rhyme without the necessity of meaning. When did sounds uncoil into letters and letters into words organized in the hierarchy of sins—venial, mortal, of omission, of commission? Of Heaven, Limbo, and Hell? Words that divide and make me wonder how I can be Catholic if I don't believe what the church teaches about the ordination of women, birth control, ecumenical communion, or homosexuality.

The priest approaches the altar for the Liturgy of the Eucharist, the part of the mass that draws on the ancient tradition of sacrificial offerings. It is a mystical dance of chants, incense, and chimes that builds to the moment when flatbread becomes the body of Christ. The organist plays the opening measures of *Panis Angelicus.* I look up to the loft and envision my mother at the pump organ accompanying Aunt Bertha, Uncle Bill, and my father, the entire choir at St. Mary's. For years after my father's death, I longed to hear his voice once more. Then, on an Easter Sunday in South Korea, two men sing *Panis Angelicus,* and a tenor holds a single, perfect note. Despite the warmth of bodies pushed against me and the stuffy air of the sanctuary, I shiver.

People leave the pews and walk toward the communion railing. I haven't received communion for some time out of respect for Church doctrine, or perhaps more truthfully, out of guilt. But today celebrates the resurrection, when everything seems possible, and time scuttles backwards to Christmas Eve in 1968 when I hear my mother whisper to my Methodist husband, "You have every right to receive the Eucharist." In matters of Church teachings, Mother was often unpredictable. "Unbaptised babies left in Limbo? How ridiculous," she said. "God wouldn't leave babies out of Heaven. And furthermore, all good people go to Heaven. Doesn't matter what church they attend." So I was both surprised and yet not surprised when she led Ken to the communion railing that night. I feel her behind me now as I walk toward the priest who holds a gold *ciborium* in one hand, a wafer pinched between the fingers of the other. I place the host on my tongue.

After mass, the choir director stands in the corner of the foyer, and I approach him, saying, "Your choir makes it possible to believe in the resurrection." The next week as I walk back from communion, he stands in the loft smiling and waving above his head compact discs recorded by the choir. The Hangul on the back cover shapes swallow's wings and flowing grasses into words I can't interpret. But tucked between the Hangul characters are familiar words—*Gounoud, Verdi, Domine Jesu Christie*—which blur into new words I'm learning—*zazen, dharma, samadhi*. I often listen to these compact discs to ease my homesickness for the church I have loved.

On Ascension Thursday I walk under a swallowtail roof suspended on columns and painted in vivid images of dragons, lotus blossoms, and lanterns. This is the gate leading to the statue of Tongil Daebul, the Great Unification Buddha located in the heart of the Taebaek Mountain Range in Seoraksan National Park. Just a few miles away from here, a fence divides families and two nations. This statue was conceived and constructed in the hopes this fence would be torn down. But the people still wait.

I hike for several minutes fretting that I have misread the guidebook and am following the wrong path when suddenly a massive image of Buddha emerges through the trees. At sixty feet high, Tongil Daebul, a gilt-bronze statue of Buddha sitting cross-legged on a lotus blossom, is the largest statue of a sitting Buddha in South Korea. His hands shape the *mudra* of enlightenment. A lotus flower of rhinestones or crystals glitters from the middle of his forehead, and a halo woven of sea-green metal rods radiates in a half circle around his head. There is serenity in the lines of his hooded eyes, full lips that nearly smile, and hands relaxed on his lap. I feel the tension in my shoulders loosen. I breathe more slowly.

I grew up kneeling in the shadow of Christ's suffering, nails in his hands and feet and ribs poking through flesh. In grade school Catechism class, Sister told us not to worry because Christ had power over death. "He could rip those nails from his hands and feet the way he moved the stone on Easter and rose to Heaven." She gave us holy cards with a picture of Jesus sitting on a throne in a shimmering light which she said was God. "He is at home with his father," she said. Sometimes that comforted me. But often, her words couldn't ease the sorrow I felt when I saw the tear tracking down Christ's cheek.

I slip out of my shoes and walk across a concrete square, past people kneeling on pillows and murmuring prayers. Bags of rice lean against the base of an altar below the statue, offerings for an abundant life. A cupboard with glass doors holds large candles. The flames flicker in the reflection. There is no railing like the communion railing in St. Mary's to separate worshipers from the altar below Buddha. It feels both strange and right to be so close that I could touch the altar's gilt-bronze top, could trace the lotus flowers carved in the panels below it.

I follow monks as they walk in meditation over a stone bridge that spans a ravine. When we reach Sinheungsa Temple, the oldest Zen temple in Korea, I don't go into the hall where they will pray. I sit on a bench with my face to the sun. The snow shimmers through the mist covering the hilltops, and a piney breeze drifts through the valley. The chants of monks echo over the mountains, bringing memories of my father echoing the priest: *Kyrie, eleison, Christe, eleison.*

This place is what the Celts called a thin place, where the border between the temporal and the spiritual world collapses, a place where shamanists might dance under trees, calling on Sanshin, the mountain god, to protect them. Shamanism, Museok Jonggyo, is a belief that spirits inhabit the living world, and it blurs the line between the natural and human worlds. I feel that sense of communion now. Bells ringing from the temple are the songs of birds. The monks' chants are the wind lifting at daybreak and fading at dusk. In my childhood church, the outdoors became the indoors. There was the smell of dirt and grass in summer, silage and crisp air in autumn, wet wool and manure in winter, and in spring the loamy aroma of winter wheat sprouting through soil. The morning sun streamed through St. Mary's stained glass windows and bathed the chapel in rainbows. Peppery-smelling incense spiraled upward and dispersed into wisps of clouds that trailed across the ceiling.

Thomas Aquinas asked if I were Catholic or Christian. It's a question I still can't answer. Where is my spiritual home?

Perhaps it's nowhere. Perhaps it's everywhere. In stained glass windows and flickering candles, in sage and drum songs on river bluffs, in the silence of a simple room and a stone-arched mosque or synagogue, under the trees dancing with the shamans and rattling paper birds over my head. A gong is struck once, twice, three times. I plant my feet to root myself in the earth and shape a circle with my fingers. I close my eyes and breathe—in and out, deep and slow.

Dusk begins to settle over the mountains, and I leave the bench and walk back down the path and over the bridge. I stop at the base of Tongil Daebul, place my hands together, press them to my breasts, and bow. What would my high school friends call me now? Infidel? Heretic? Pagan? But Catholic children understand metaphor. I didn't pray to the plaster of Paris Madonna nor do I now pray to the bronze Buddha. It is the lines, textures, and colors in the statues and paintings that inspire me; the fragrances, light, and music that move me. Even a child, perhaps especially a child, can sense the harmony in the way that sensuousness and spirituality are entwined like morning glory vines wrapped around our fence posts, their lavender blossoms open to the sun.

Chapter Eleven

Eunhee crosses her legs and jiggles her foot. The sequins on her sandal straps sparkle in the sunlight, but they do not brighten the mood in the room.

"I am so unhappy because I gained weight in college," she says. "Mother is a dancer and thin like Madonna and Britney. She pinches my fat and makes me weigh every day."

She is by most standards a slight woman with small breasts, narrow hips, and slim waist. She looks even tinier in an oversized chair and more like a child in a blouse with a Peter Pan collar trimmed in pink satin. She wears daisy-covered barrettes in her black hair.

In eighth grade, I gained twenty pounds. Worst of all, my breasts "blossomed," a *Seventeen* magazine word that didn't describe how the buttons strained against my blouses and opened gaps that exposed my bra. Clothes that fit me were matronly-looking. I used rubber bands to keep my hair out of my eyes.

Eunhee chews on her bottom lip, says nothing for a moment, and then begins to sob, "I hate myself because I eat bread and cookies at bakeries all the time."

Young women like Eunhee come to my office for conversation hour and quickly begin to speak of their career dreams and their frustration with a patriarchal culture that changes too slowly for them. They complain of mothers who stay home and fathers who let their wives care for his parents, of old Confucian expectations that women be silent and compliant. I'm not certain why they are so open with me. Maybe because they know I will be in Korea for only a few months, they trust their stories will leave with me. Maybe the intimacy of the baths creates an intimacy among women in general. Perhaps because of television shows like *Friends*, which many of the young women watch, they assume all Americans share their private thoughts in public ways. Whatever the reason, they come and they talk and very often the conversation turns to their unhappiness with what they see in the mirror.

Gloria's black eyes glisten as she struggles to explain why she longs for a surgery that would stitch a permanent crease in her single-lidded eyes.

"I beg my parents to take me to Make Over Town," she laments.

Make Over Town is a Seoul neighborhood filled with plastic surgery clinics, including one that is eighteen stories high where doctors perform two hundred eye surgeries a day. I envisioned surgeons draped in white, only their eyes above surgical masks exposed. I saw gurneys carrying women through brightly lit operating rooms with the efficiency of a conveyor belt in a factory as doctors made quick tiny slits in their eyes.

Gloria pops out of her chair, walks to the mirror, and props open her eyes with her fingers. "Like this. But they say no. If I have round eyes then nobody will laugh because I am ugly."

Honey complains that she is too short. "In Korea, if you change your height you can change your future. I will get a better job if I am taller."

She brings a copy of *The Seoul Times* with pictures of little girls sitting on metal tables, acupuncture needles poking out around their mouths, limbs, and abdomens while a nurse injects them with growth hormones. Other girls caged in wire-and-canvas harnesses walk on treadmills. Weights attached to the harnesses pull on their backs and legs to stretch their spines.

"It's too late for me," Honey says. "I am too old to grow any more. I should have had the treatments when I was a child. Then I would be tall and beautiful like an American model."

Susie frets about her skin tone. "I buy creams like Whitelight, Future Whiten Day, White Perfect, Blanc Purette, but I am still too dark."

She wants to have laser treatments and surgeries that promise to lighten her coffee-colored complexion. "Koreans say that one white covers up three uglinesses."

I remind her about tanning booths in America and girls who line the beaches, lying in the sun until their skin turns bronze. She ignores me. She hands me a tube of skin lightener. When I open the lid, I smell a hint of something chemical. I wonder if she knows or cares that women who have no money for expensive creams buy lotions with mercuric chloride that often leave them horribly disfigured.

*　　　*　　　*

"I wish you knew me when I was thin and pretty," Eunhee says. She digs in her purse, pulls out a wad of tissues, and wipes the tears pooling in the corners of her dark eyes. "Now I am sad and have no confidence. I am all alone and have no friends."

I tell Eunhee about the day I became a fat girl.

I was humming "Will You Still Love Me Tomorrow?" a tune my friends and I played endlessly, dropping quarters in a miniature jukebox attached to the wall in our booth at the Rainbow Café. The record rose and flipped, showering our faces in neon. We dipped French fries in ketchup, sipped cherry Cokes, and giggled with the excitement of being freshmen in high school, a year that seemed filled with possibilities for me. But this year I would lose weight, make the cheerleading squad, and then maybe the boy with crinkly eyes would notice me.

I met a family friend as I stepped out of the restaurant under an afternoon sky of cornflower blue and air that smelled of clean linens.

She said, "Hi, Jeanne."

My sister, Jeanne, was slender with long legs and a tiny waist. She carried herself with my father's impeccable posture, her shoulders back, head high. Her breasts were barely visible beneath the cardigan sweaters she buttoned down the back. I wore oversized sweatshirts and hunched my shoulders to pull in my chest. I kept my head lowered.

I corrected her. "No, I'm Mary Alice."

"Oh, that's right," she said. "Jeanne's the thin sister."

That night I began my campaign for diet pills, amphetamines readily prescribed by doctors in those days.

"You're not heavy," my mother objected. "You have a nice shape. I don't want you taking pills you don't need."

I pouted at the supper table, clomped around the house, refusing to speak, and spent hours in my bedroom, sulking. Finally, perhaps persuaded that my happiness depended on the pills—or, more likely, exhausted from dealing with my moodiness—my mother relented and made an appointment with the doctor.

"I thought that pills would make me thin and happy," I tell Eunhee. "But instead they made me anxious and sleepless, and so I ate more and gained more weight."

When my mother saw my hollow eyes and shaky hands, she threw the pills in the toilet and stormed out of the bathroom, her mouth pinched and her eyes flashing. She was probably angry at herself for giving in and at me for being so insistent.

That night I sat on my bed in a dimly lit room, my hair rolled in Coke cans. There was a pile of Hershey Kisses wrappers near me, their foil glittering in the street light shining through the window. I knew my mother and I would never again speak of my weight. As the chocolate melted over my tongue, I could taste pleasure mixed with disgust, resolve with failure.

Eunhee weeps quietly. Then she says, "I wish I had diet pills. Or else could starve myself."

I lean across the coffee table to take her hand, but she tucks her head into her shoulder, pulls her knees to her chest, and curls into a knot. Her hair falls over her face and muffles her sobs.

I walk to the window and look at the mountains dappled with light and shadows in the sunlight weaving through the clouds. I imagine Koreans, perhaps even Eunhee's grandparents, darting through the trees, hiding from soldiers, gnawing on bark and stuffing blades of grass into their dry mouths. When the war ended, these emaciated Koreans filled their empty stomachs with rice, vegetables, and meat, and pointed with pride to their pounds, proof of their prosperity. Now many of their granddaughters, skeletal as refugees, starve themselves or crouch in bathroom stalls to purge, and eating disorders clinics and fat camps proliferate over the Korean peninsula.

Perhaps that's why Mother, a child of the Depression, was so offended by thin people. Like those Koreans who survived war and starvation, she'd had her fill of doing without. When she spotted a picture of Audrey Hepburn I'd ripped out of *Modern Screen* and taped to my bedroom wall, she snorted, "She could use a few pounds. Look at those chicken legs." Mother saw no value in going hungry for vanity's sake.

She scolded grown children for drinking diet sodas and skipping desserts. She scoffed at the notion of limiting her grandchildren's sugar intake. "A bit of sugar can't hurt," she said as she pulled Dilly Bars and ice cream sandwiches from the freezer, Twinkies and Oreo cookies from the cupboard. The grandchildren crowded around her like baby chicks at a feeder. Mother smiled as she watched them pecking at the sweets with their sharp little teeth. I detected a glint of triumph in her eyes.

In her later years, when her hair was the color of November leaves on cottonwood trees and her skin unfolded in accordion pleats from her bones, she looked in the mirror and lamented the loss of her once generous hips and bosom. "Why do people want to look like this?"

"Mother scold me because I sneak to Kentucky Fried Chicken and eat chicken strips and hot wings," Eunhee says. She sniffs her sleeve. "My clothes smell like grease, so she will know I ate fried chicken. She will yell at me tonight."

She squeezes her tiny hands into fists and kneads the flesh of her thighs with her knuckles—hard, as if to punish herself.

What would it be like to have a mother monitor your weight as Eunhee's mother did? To have a mother obsessed with each pound you gained? My mother was never critical of my body. She often complimented me on how pretty I looked and how my dresses and haircuts flattered me. But what else could a mother say? And how could her reassurances compete with Sandra Dee and Annette Funicello, skinny little women with heads too big for their bodies and the voices of little girls. The girls I wanted to be.

For a time, I bought clothes too small, and they left red marks where they pinched my skin. Then I bought clothes too large, so that I looked even bulkier. I avoided mirrors. My senior year in college, I met Ken. He was the first man I knew who wasn't an athlete but worked out every day. We took long walks at night. Once in a while I even jogged around the track with him and lifted hand weights in his apartment. He grilled lean steaks and baked potatoes for us. I gave up keg parties. I lost thirty pounds. Still I see the face of a miserable fat girl whenever I look in the mirror.

Eunhee jumps out of the chair and walks to the door. Then she stops and says into the door. "I'm ashamed I cried in front of my professor." She leaves before I can say anything to her. The smell of fried chicken lingers in the room.

Chicken sizzled in a skillet of lard, and the temperature inched toward the nineties as the prairie wind blasted hot air through the windows in our farmhouse. I sorted and washed eggs I had gathered that morning while Mother prepared dinner for the members of her Take Off Pounds Sensibly Club.

Sweat tracked through the flour that dusted my mother's cheeks, and her ankles swelled with the heat. She brought a floor fan into the kitchen, draped a wet towel over it, and hiked the back hem of her housedress into the belt beneath her ample bosom, making her dress Russian

Cossack pants that ballooned above her knees. They fluttered in the air that blew across her legs.

My mother belonged to many groups—Whist Club, Home Extension, Altar Society, and the Emily Dickinson Club, which she fled the afternoon a member read "Because I Could Not Stop for Death."

"I think that poet was seriously depressed," Mother declared.

But her membership in TOPS was the strangest. She resisted the club's mission of weight loss and ignored the rules the way she ignored the scout leader's guidebook for conducting Brownie meetings. Once we finished the flag ceremony and the Pledge of Allegiance, she let the troop chase each other in games of musical chairs, beanies sailing over the room and socks drooping around our ankles, while she played "Rock Around the Clock" and "Great Balls of Fire" on the upright in the basement of the Lutheran church. A shoebox with yarn, glue, sacks of macaroni, and colors sat on the bench beside her. We never completed a project. But which of us wild girls would complain?

For my family, TOPS night was a rare evening of company that wasn't family. For the members, who had mostly lost and gained the same twenty pounds during the year, it was a respite from the battle they waged with the scale. I think for Mother it was a covert campaign against the group's goals.

When I think of TOPS night, I imagine Mother sitting on the stoop of our farm house as she fanned her dimpled thighs with the hem of her housedress, absent-mindedly rubbing the blue veins that collided at her ankles. She tilted her head as she listened for the whine of tires coming down the dirt lane.

Living on the grasslands, we had grown accustomed to the silence broken only occasionally by the bellowing of a calf or gears shifting on a gravel road a quarter mile to the east. It was an isolation that my father loved. He didn't want to see and hear neighbors. "Might as well live in town," he said, which of course we eventually did. My mother, however, admired the clusters of yard lights we saw as we drove east down Highway 16. "Those lights are like stars," she said. "They make the skies seem kinda friendly, don't they?"

On TOPS night, my mother slaughtered chickens with slashes of an ax through bone and cartilage. I chased a headless chicken, laughing at the spastic gait of its scrawny, yellow legs as it ran around the yard. I was unnerved and thrilled by the bloody stump above the feathers. She plunged the chickens into buckets of boiling water, plucked the feathers, and singed the pin feathers over the gas flame of the stove. As she quartered the birds with thrusts of a knife, did she imagine how the women might moan as they chewed on the crisp, succulent flesh? How they might savor even the marrow of thigh bones? When Mother was done slaughtering, her hands were covered in white fluff and bits of burgundy-colored organ meat, and although she washed them in hot water and Lava soap, they smelled of wet feathers and burnt flesh.

Four cars careened into our farmyard, raising dust that drifted in sparkling columns across the yard. Several women—some pear- or apple-shaped, and some whose fleshy calves surrendered to thick ankles—tumbled out of the cars laughing. They invaded our kitchen, where platters of chicken fried to a golden crust, bowls of mashed potatoes and gravy, corn on the cob, caramel rolls oozing with butter and brown sugar, lime gelatin dotted with cottage cheese, and flaky-crusted pies stretched over the kitchen counter like creeping jenny over the sidewalk. The women stacked food on plates and stormed into the yard to hunker down in bulging lawn chairs.

Mother walked around the yard, pouring lemonade, offering slices of apple pie she'd made that morning. The pies infused the house with the aromas of cinnamon and sugar, flour and tart fruit.

"We're not getting on the scale tonight, gals, so have a couple slices."

After the women had picked the plates clean, they walked into our house for the TOPS meeting. I went to my bedroom to read, but I could hear their chattering in the living room.

The treasurer rattled off numbers. "We took in two hundred forty-five dollars in dues and one hundred and twenty-five in fines for a total of three hundred and seventy dollars. We sent national dues of two hundred dollars, leaving a balance of one hundred and seventy. Expenses for the year included one hundred dollars to the Rainbow Café for the annual Christmas party, and fifteen dollars to the Chamberlain Bakery for the cookies for the Valentine's Day party."

Next, the secretary, who recorded the pounds lost and gained by the members during the year, presented a balance sheet of another sort: "As a group, we lost three hundred and thirty-three pounds this year and gained two hundred and twenty-five. But that's an improvement over last year's record."

"And now," the president said, "I'm pleased to announce that the big loser for this year is Dorothy, who lost eleven and a half pounds." The women cheered.

As the grand loser, Dorothy was responsible for TIPS for TOPS. "Well," she said, "the tip I have is something I learned from an article I read in *Ladies Home Journal.* I bought this small notebook,"—she held up a notebook the size of a deck of cards—"and I carry it with me everywhere so I can write down everything I eat that day and..."

By now, the women were hopped up on caffeine and sugar and began to squirm in their chairs. Mother made her move.

"Humph, a notebook that size, I could fill up one page just writing down what I had for breakfast." The other members giggled as they calculated how many pages of the notebook each would need to keep count of her daily intake.

Mother advanced her cause. "Maybe we should designate a different letter of the alphabet for each day and write down only those foods we ate that day that begin with that letter."

A perfect comedic pause. "Like we could have a C-food day and write down things like chocolate cake and cherry pie à la mode."

The meeting ended without a motion to adjourn as the women gathered for a song. Amidst the laughter, Mother's fingers sailed over the piano keys, and I went into the living room and lay on the floor to watch the fun. In the same spirit with which armies march to bagpipes and drums after battles, Mother celebrated the triumph of her evening with music. Her hips spread across the stool, and one foot beat time on the floor while the other pumped the loud pedal.

Nimble in spite of their bulk, the women lifted their skirts above their knees and danced the Charleston across the living room linoleum, fleshy thighs rippling. "I'll be down to get you in a taxi, Honey."

They paired off and did the Lindy, twirling one another so rapidly their rhinestone earrings sparkled like snow in moonlight. One woman lifted me off the floor, and we romped around the room until I was short of breath from twirling and dizzy with the smell of Evening in Paris and perspiration. She dropped me in a chair and then jitterbugged by herself, her arms flying over her head, her feet zigging and zagging around one another. Mother laughed and began to play the bass notes with a wild syncopation that made the women spin more feverishly.

What would Eunhee's mother, that pencil-thin ballerina, think of such women whose weight must have tripled her own? Could she have imagined women who frolicked with such wild abandon? Years later when only her memories could dance, Mother would say to me, "Do you remember when I invited the TOPS Club to dinner? I can still see those women whooping it up in the living room. Oh my, we had such fun."

Finally the heat and the dancing had exhausted them and the sweat ran down their sides to dampen the belts under their heavy breasts. They stood arm in arm around the piano, singing while my mother harmonized in her strong alto, "We'll build a sweet, little nest, somewhere in the West, and let the rest of the world go by."

As the cars drove away, Mother stood on the back stoop watching the taillights until they faded into the night. She walked back to her kitchen where dirty dishes, rumpled napkins, and chicken bones lay in piles on the table and flakes of pie crust dusted the countertop like ashes over rubble. She picked up the skillet, hauled it to the sink, and filled it with scalding water and dish powder. As she attacked the bits of flesh and fat stuck to the bottom, digging at the remains with a scouring pad, a sliver of a smile slid across her face; her hazel eyes beneath their heavy lids danced.

CHAPTER TWELVE

I scissor my chopsticks, seize a clump of *baechu kimchi,* bring it to my nose, and sniff.

"What does it smell like?" Ken asks.

"Hmm, not sure," I say, sniffing again.

We are having lunch in a *kkape,* a cozy café overlooking a street in Gung Dong with pubs, boutiques, and coffee shops. Earlier, a gray-haired gentleman in a nubby cardigan and corduroy pants met us at the door, bowed, and led us to a low Korean table in a sunny corner. I assumed he was the owner.

He handed us menus printed in Hangul and waited, order pad and pencil in hand. Although I had memorized a few foods from a travel guidebook, I couldn't read the menu, so I pointed to a line of characters. He frowned and shook his head. I tried another line. Another frown. Finally, when I pointed at still another line of Hangul, he bowed, grinned, and said, "Okay. Okay."

Now he returns carrying a tray with two metal bowls of *bap,* and several ceramic bowls of *banchan,* a variety of side dishes: doilies of pickled lotus root, wriggling cubes of caramel-colored acorn jelly, seaweed roasted with tawny sesame oil, slices of grilled sweet potatoes, and two kinds of *kimchi*—yellow daikon radish and red cabbage *kimchi.* I nibble a piece of the red cabbage and bite into a sliver of chili pepper. A grass fire flashes across my bottom lip. "Yikes. This is hot."

The man scurries back to our table and points to the bowl of *kimchi,* his eyebrows raised. "*Mashieoptta?*" (Not delicious?) I shake my head. "*Anyo, mashiitta.*" (No, it's good.) I blink back the tears pooling beneath my lashes from the sour heat of the cabbage. I hear my mother's voice in my head, *I coulda told ya not take that bite, but you had to try it.*

"Okay, okay," the man says and wanders off to another table.

While Ken and I wait for our meal, we squirm to find a comfortable position. I try the lotus position for about ten minutes before my legs cramp. I pull one leg up to my chest, bend the other leg under my bottom, and sit on the diagonal at the table. Ken grabs a leg and wraps it over the other one like a pretzel. But when he straightens his back, he nearly tips over. So he pulls himself close to the table and stretches his legs underneath. Koreans consider it rude to straighten your legs while you eat, but they forgive foreigners for this breech of etiquette. The eyes of the other diners twinkle at the sight of his stocking feet sticking up beneath the table.

The gentleman brings stone pots filled with rice and topped with slivers of beef, julienne cuts of raw zucchini and carrots, and sautéed mushrooms. A fried egg with a dollop of *gochu-jang*, hot red pepper paste, slides down the mound of rice like lava down a volcano's side. He takes my chopsticks, mixes the toppings into the rice, bows, and leaves. The pots are so hot that the rice on the bottom sizzles while we eat. He has introduced us to *dolsot bibimbap*, the house specialty, a dish so delicious that I have since driven two hours to a town in South Dakota where a Korean woman serves this in her restaurant.

I take another bite of *kimchi*, this time chewing slowly, being mindful as Buddha taught of everything infused in this bit of food—the crunch of cabbage, the greens slippery in my mouth, the tart taste of ginger, and a hint of apple or pear. I see the tendons in the women's fingers tighten as they slide a knife through cabbage. My hands are their hands working the ingredients into a paste and spreading it over the leaves. I feel the warmth of the sun against the farmer's back as he works in the rice fields and harvests salt in the marshes along the sea. I am everything—farmer, woman, earth, and sea.

I sniff the *kimchi* again. There is a hint of fish oil and vinegar, fragrances that provoke a memory of sitting at a kitchen table with my father, eating sardines and pickled herring on rye crackers. My mother watched us, her eyes narrowed, lips puckered. "How can you eat that slop?"

My father had an eclectic appetite and, because I was a bit in love with him, the way little girls often are, I wanted to mimic him, even at the cost of irritating my mother. We layered beef heart or dimpled slices of boiled tongue between white bread slathered with butter; gnawed on pickled pig's feet, the pearly knuckles poking through pink muscle; and sipped sauerkraut juice mixed with tomato juice. At that kitchen table, I became obsessed with food—

the colors and textures on the plate, its flavors and fragrances, and its fusion of memories of other times and other meals.

Korean cuisine is a kaleidoscope of complimentary colors, tastes, smells, and textures—red, green, yellow, white, and black; vegetables, grains, meats, and seafood; sweet and salty, hot and cold, spicy and mild, vinegary and fishy.

In Korea, I gobbled every dish offered to me—*boolgogi*, grilled sliced beef with tastes of soy sauce, sesame oil, garlic, and sugar; *dwaeji galbi*, pork ribs marinated in crushed pears, chili paste, garlic, and malt syrup, grilled over charcoal, and wrapped in crisp lettuce leaves; *ggoti gomthang*, oxtail soup with slivers of green onion in a white broth; and *haemul jongol*, seafood hot pots cooked in cast-iron pots on table-top grills. With nearly every bite I heard Mother complain, *What's wrong with good old fashioned American food?*

If I immersed myself in Korean cuisine as a way to experience its culture, Mother may have refused to eat "foreign foods" as a way to cling to her Irish heritage. Ethnicity mattered when I was a child. On the first day of school, the teacher walked down the aisle, handing out a sheet of paper with squares next to a list of nationalities— Irish, Scottish, English, Russian, German, French, Bohemian. I don't remember a square for Native American. "Blacken the squares that identify your heritage," the teacher said. "If you don't know, you may take it home to your parents and bring it back tomorrow."

I don't know why we took the survey. Nor do I know who needed the information. But none of us had to take the paper home. We knew our countries of origin. There were still traces of ethnic settlements in my home county when I was young. North of Reliance was the Bohemian neighborhood with names like Bucacek, Straka, Ptacek, (my paternal grandmother's name), and Woster, which my ancestors changed from Vostrejs when they came to America. South and west were the Irish—Cullen (my maternal grandmother's name), Donelan, O'Donnell, and McManus (my mother's maiden name).

But I didn't know much about the cuisine of my heritage. When I was growing up, the food my mother prepared was delicious, but mostly pale and bland—fried chicken, mashed potatoes and gravy, corn on the cob, fresh-baked bread, and apple pie, the best I've ever tasted. It was the yin and yang of pastry. A firm crust that flaked at the touch of a fork, sugar balanced against pungent cinnamon, the hint of green fruit in a white crust.

I don't remember Norwegians in our county, so I didn't know about their cuisine until I married Ken. From him I learned about *krub*, a potato dumpling wrapped around a piece of pork or ham that his mother baked one day and then sliced and fried in lard the next. "She wasn't afraid of grease," he jokes. He didn't eat *lefse* and *lutefisk*, although I have tried both, but he remembers with pleasure the platters of *rosettes*, *krumkake*, and *fattigman* that his Aunt Inga delivered every Christmas. Over the years, I've cooked *saurbraten* and red cabbage and served brats and pickled herring. I've baked pastry with almond filling. My motive was less to celebrate Ken's German heritage than my curiosity about how those foods tasted, how the colors brightened the plate, and how the fragrances of bay leaf and juniper berries, onion and beef, sugar and butter perfumed my kitchen.

My brown-eyed grandchildren would need two sheets of paper with boxes to mark their heritages—Irish, Bohemian, German, Norwegian, English, Scottish, French, and Cherokee, and perhaps others. Maybe I should expand my culinary repertoire to include *wojapi* wrapped in crepes and bannock with lamb shanks, haggis and shepherds pie, chokecherry tea and café au lait, oatcakes and beignets, Yorkshire Pudding and *tuyagadu*, bean bread.

In the way that farm and ranch women once gathered to can meat or vegetables for the winter, Korean women came together to make *kimchi*, mixing red-pepper-flecked chunks of cabbage wide and rippled as ribbon candy, fiery chili pods, blackish mustard greens, bits of dusty-yellow ginger root, fish oil, and crushed apple. I like to imagine little girls on *kimchi* day listening to their mothers and aunties tell stories as they chop and dice, and mix and layer the ingredients in clay pots as big as umbrella stands. I see them following the women to the backyard to bury the pots so the cabbage can ferment.

Generations of mothers and daughters are embedded in the stories that women tell as they work in the kitchen. I remember a Christmas Eve long ago when I was a little girl sitting at the kitchen counter eating cinnamon toast. Mother's voice joined the rattle of lids on simmering pots and the parakeet chirping in the corner. Perhaps it was in the spirit of the season that she prepared a meal to appease my father's central European tastes, or possibly it gave her a chance to complain about her Bohemian in-laws' culinary customs.

"Your Grandfather Woster used to smoke hams in the shed out back," my mother said. "Then he hung the ham from the kitchen ceiling. And if you can believe this, he would walk over to that ham, whack off a chunk with his knife, and eat it right then and there. Yuk."

She poured milk and a bit of cream into a stockpot and plopped oysters into the milk. "Issh, these things stink. Ya know, there was always something smelly in the Woster house, like sauerkraut fermenting in crocks or blood sausage on the stove."

She didn't know how much I longed to smell that sausage, to taste it, and feel the crumbly texture in my mouth. Years later at a bed and breakfast in Ireland, I did eat blood sausage along with rashers, fried eggs and tomatoes, chewy brown bread, porridge laced with whisky, and tea with milk and sugar which I slurped from a saucer.

"Did I ever tell you about the time your father took me to dinner at a Bohemian café on our honeymoon in Omaha? They served some kinda meat that was soaked in vinegar with green leafy things and parsnips and mushrooms and hot red pepper. Issh."

I imagine my mother, a shy bride pretending to like *svickova* and *jaeger schnitzel* while vowing to never eat such foreign food again. A vow she kept for over sixty years. But she put aside her disgust for foreign foods when it came to breads. "I learned to make *kolaches* from your dad's Aunt Bessie when we stayed at her house in Omaha."

Mother slapped a ball of dough on a flour-dusted countertop, raising flecks that spiraled through the shaft of light shining through the window. She plopped the dough in a greased bowl and covered it with a flour sack. While the dough rose, she mixed apricots with water and sugar, and let the fruit simmer. Mother smiled as she rolled the dough into balls smooth as mushrooms, filled the centers with stewed apricots.

She stopped her work and looked up at me, "Aunt Bessie was a tall, elegant woman, and I was a little afraid of her because she spoke mostly Bohemian. It was gibberish to me. But her breads were beautiful and golden, and the texture so velvety."

Later she took the *kolaches* out of the oven and put them on the counter to cool. In the winter sun streaming through the window, they were amber broaches wrapped in gold. "We were married on Valentine's Day. The department store windows were filled with cardboard cutouts of red and white hearts and bouquets of paper flowers."

She walked to the sink, picked up a bar of Ivory soap, and turned it over and over in her hands. The suds dripped through her fingers as she gazed out the window to the spot where the snow-frosted prairie grasses met the winter sky.

"Those windows were the prettiest things I'd ever seen."

When ill health forced Mother's move to an assisted-living facility in Sioux Falls, two hundred miles east of where she had lived for over eighty years, she left her family, neighbors, and her history. "The hardest thing about moving here isn't leaving my house and giving away my things. It is that nobody knows anything about Lyman County—your dad, the farm, you kids, my parents and siblings. They don't know any of the important things about me."

It was a difficult transition, but my mother somehow summoned the courage to build a new life. She strolled down the halls and stopped at open doors to chat. She played bingo, although she never learned to like the game, and signed up for the Out-To-Lunch-Bunch, a group of women who took the bus every week to a different restaurant. She remained a member until her death.

One night, she told me that the lunch bunch had eaten at the Golden Bowl. "I had their almond chicken and it was so good." I recalled a night years ago when I took her to a Chinese restaurant and she ate nothing but rice—no soy sauce, not even a sliver of meat or vegetable. She spent the dinner staring at the plate in stony silence.

"Mother," I said, "you don't like Chinese food. Remember how annoyed you were when I took you to Hunan's? You wouldn't the touch the food."

"Oh, that's ridiculous. I wouldn't have acted that way."

Perhaps my memory was false. In those days, I was so defensive about underlying criticism from my mother that even an innocuous remark that I felt carried an edge could season the evening with my defensiveness. Maybe that night at Hunan's she was silenced by my tension. Or maybe her memories had been softened by the years.

"Some of the women tried to use chopsticks. The food flew all over the place. It was so funny."

A little boy with Harry Potter glasses and a Dennis the Menace cowlick taught Ken and me to use chopsticks the night we ate at a restaurant in Daejeon that specialized in *samgyetang*, a soup made with a small chicken stuffed with rice and served in a bowl of broth.

"Put one chopstick between thumb and middle finger," he said. "Use the second finger on other chopstick and pick up food like scissors." His chopsticks flashed as he tugged at the chicken. The flesh fell away, and globs of rice, slices of ginseng, red dates, slivers of garlic, and ginkgo nuts plopped into the broth.

As I wrestled with the chopsticks, I heard him whisper to his mother, "She crossing top stick over bottom." The mother put her finger to her lips, "Shhhh." When I successfully picked up a piece of chicken with my twisted sticks, he clapped and said, "Very good for foreigner. You learn quickly."

Eventually, we did become proficient with chopsticks, but we still embarrassed ourselves now and then. One evening at a dinner hosted by two professors, Ken clamped down on a peanut with his chopsticks. It whizzed like a bullet across the table between them, hit the wall, bounced off, and landed on the floor next to one gentleman's shoe. They kept eating as if they hadn't noticed.

Mother had chuckled. "Whoever came up with the idea of eating with sticks anyway?" But there was no bite to her words, just puzzled amusement.

She asked me to take her to an Italian restaurant a few weeks before she died. One of her friends had raved about the mushroom risotto, and she wanted to try it. "I think I'll like it," Mother said. "It's mostly rice."

In the foyer of the restaurant was a painting of a café along a Venice canal. I remembered eating lunch with Jeanne at a table covered in white linens and crystal goblets. Yellow daisies in a ceramic vase nestled near a bottle of wine. We chatted as gondoliers in sailor pants and red-and-white striped jackets glided past us through the narrow corridor of water. "Mother, I ate pasta puttanesca and drank Orvieto wine in a café just like that."

Mother pointed to the crooked buildings in the painting. "Oh, those buildings of pink and yellow are like something in a fairy tale," she said.

She leaned closer to the picture. "Are they really standing in water like that?"

"Yes."

We stood in silence for a few minutes as she peered at the painting. What was she was thinking? Mother touched the glass where the waves lapped against the rotting foundations.

"How sad, such beautiful things slipping into the sea."

Then she clasped her hand around my elbow, and we followed the hostess through the crowded café to a booth. Her fingers trembled against my sleeve, her breath came in small gasps.

She ordered the risotto, and I ordered a bowl of mussels. When the risotto came, she pushed the rice around the plate and picked at a mushroom with her fork. "You know your father's family used to drive a team of horses down to the Missouri River bottom and gather mushrooms in the woods."

I held my breath, hoping she wouldn't stop talking. I knew so little about my father's past. My mother instilled Irish pride in her children. She sang "When Irish Eyes are Smiling" as she did the dishes or hung clothes on the line. She wiped her eyes at the memory of her father dancing the jig "on little leprechaun feet." My father, however, said little about being Bohemian for reasons I still don't understand. Maybe he was too busy working the land to obsess over his heritage. Perhaps he had nothing to cherish. In 1918, Bohemia and Moravia were swallowed up by Czechoslovakia. My father was a man without a homeland.

I tried to imagine my father as a little boy in a wool jacket and cap, riding in the back of a buckwagon. I saw my grandmother, who was tall I'm told, sitting upright next to my grandfather, a scarf covering the braid wrapped around her head, her coat buttoned to her neck. I imagined my grandfather's hair was thin, and that he wore a muffler and leather gloves on his hands wrapped around the reins. I could hear the hooves thudding against sod as the horse plodded over a trail cut through the tall grass. I could smell moss in the dark forest.

"They dried the mushrooms and stored them in the sand of the root cellar. I thought it was ridiculous to bury mushrooms in sand, and I wouldn't eat them because they smelled horrible. Besides, I was certain they would be poisonous."

She chuckled. "They looked like little shriveled ears, kinda like those mussels. But I guess that's what they liked to eat, so that's okay. Maybe I should have tried one."

She peered at the iridescent shells that floated among bits of garlic and tomatoes in a lemony butter sauce. Her eyes were narrow with curiosity, or perhaps suspicion.

"What do they taste like?"

"They're hard to describe—maybe like oysters. They're delicious," I said.

In her later years, Mother seemed to be more open to whatever life had to offer, even—I wanted to believe—a willingness to experiment with foods she once would have found repugnant. I watched as she reached into the broth, pinched a mussel shell between her fingers, plucked the flesh out of the shell, and popped it in her mouth. She smacked her lips softly as she chewed. "Hmmmn. I'm not sure about this."

Then she picked up another mussel, curled her tongue around it, and pulled it into her mouth. I was thrilled to see her eating shellfish. I imagined the foods that might have blended my heritage at our kitchen table on that farm years ago—*svickova, veprova pecene, cervene zel, sunka plnina koenovou slehavekou, colcannon, coddle, boxty,* and *barmbrack.* I mourned the meals my mother and I might have shared in distant places—espresso and foie gras in Paris, *skyr* and *pylsur* in Reykjavik, *bibimbap* and *samgyetang* in Seoul.

She looked up at me, eyebrows furrowed. "They taste like mud. Yuk. Why do you eat such slop?"

She forked a small bit of rice, brought it to her mouth, and chewed slowly. We ate the rest of the meal in silence.

Chapter Thirteen

"Do you ever feel like. . .what is the word? Nobody sees you?"

Curled up in an oversized chair, Bora looks like a child in her denim skirt over leggings, a lacy shrug, and sandals with plastic flowers on the straps. But beneath her bashful smile is a woman who smolders with frustration.

Bora signed up for conversation hour often during the semester. Sometimes I chose the topics to discuss—idioms, syntax, appropriate greetings in the work place, or American cuisine and dining customs. Other times I let her control the flow of conversation.

One day, Bora came to my office with cups of latte and almond cakes. We sipped the coffee and picked at cake crumbs with our fingers as we chatted about her coursework. But this last question drove our conversation into new territory.

"Do you mean invisible?"

She nods her head. "*Yeh.* Invisible."

Invisible: incapable by nature of being seen; inaccessible to view.

Invisible: growing up in a place so culturally and geographically insignificant that in 1989, the editors at Rand McNally omitted three states—Oklahoma, South Dakota and North Dakota—from its *Photographic World Atlas.* I didn't see the atlas, but I often imagined the borders of Minnesota, Iowa, Nebraska, Montana, and Wyoming collapsing into the void where South Dakota should have been, thereby erasing the people and places of my childhood.

"Why do you feel invisible, Bora?"

She studies the polish on her nails, worries a cuticle for a moment before saying, "People say that women shouldn't work after they get married. They say we should be 'inside-the-house persons' like our mothers."

The term "inside-the-house persons" dates back to a time when men and women lived in separate quarters in *hanok* villages like the one we toured near Seoul. It was typical of villages of the Joseon period. A wall of straw and dirt enclosed buildings with tiled roofs and thick wooden doors carved in geometric patterns. A rectangular *mandang*, or cobblestone courtyard, sat between the *Sarangchae*, the quarters where men gathered to talk politics, write poetry, and play instruments, and the *Anchae*, the inner quarters where women cooked, gossiped, gave birth, and prepared bodies for burial. The women rarely left their quarters.

In many village courtyards there was a wooden teeter-totter. Legend says that a woman would sit on one end of the board while another jumped hard on the opposite end, lifting the board high enough that the other woman could see beyond the dirt wall. I like to imagine her skirt swirling around her waist, braids flying, and eyes wide at her first glimpse of the outside world.

Husbands even slept in separate quarters from their wives, curled around bolsters called "bamboo wives" to keep them warm, except on nights when they crossed the courtyard to visit their wives or concubines. The women had no bamboo husbands. Perhaps they shared beds with other women. Or maybe wrapping their arms around a bamboo husband suggested a sexuality that proper women should not possess.

"Mother stays home all the time," Bora says. "Nobody ever sees her. She like the women years ago who veiled their faces and rode in, what do you call the carriages?" She meant palanquins, human-powered box cars.

"But I won't be home all day doing housework. I'm going to have a career and I'm going to travel."

There was no visible wall surrounding Mrs. Chang, a PhD in genetic engineering who works six days a week, fifty-one weeks a year in a research facility. We met her the night we dined at the Chang's home in a valley overlooking a lotus pond and willow trees.

Mr. Chang, a slender man with salt-and-pepper hair and an easy smile, entertained us in a cozy living room with furniture upholstered in floral chintz and walls lined with shelves of books. We sipped Sauvignon Blanc and munched on strawberries and grape tomatoes. In the kitchen Mrs. Chang, elegant in a silk tunic and slacks, chopped vegetables and fried beef.

He admitted that as a college professor, he had the more flexible schedule with frequent breaks in his classes and weekends off. "But my work is outside the home. She cares for inside," he said. "Korea is still a Confucian country that divides the lives of women from those of men, and the division of labor is grounded in that tradition." I tried not to judge him or impose western standards on their marriage, but I was irritated with him.

When we sat down for dinner, Mrs. Chang stayed in the kitchen. I couldn't help asking, "Mrs. Chang, will you join us at the table?"

"No, that's fine. I'll eat after you leave." Her voice lacked the resentment I sometimes feel when Ken is not as helpful as I expect him to be.

As we drove home that night, I wondered if I imposed tensions that didn't exist onto this couple. They smiled warmly at one another as she leaned over to refill his wine glass, touching his shoulder in the way women who love their husbands do. Bora may not yet understand the compromises and agreements that couples make in marriage.

"One day I will own a restaurant and then I will wear fancy clothes and buy a beautiful apartment with expensive"—Bora points to the chairs—"*kagu*." She gets up and paces the floor.

"Nobody will keep me from being a business woman, not even my *nampyeon*. You would say husband. He can't tell me what to do."

Suddenly I learn that Bora is married. I look out the window so she doesn't see the surprise in my eyes. I don't want her to stop talking.

"My husband only sees me as a caretaker for his parents. He says they will move in with us one day, and because I am his *anae*, I must stay home and care for them. He complains because I don't call his mother every day. I have things to do. Besides, she does not own me."

Korean women were once seen as property of their husbands' families, often treated like slaves by their mothers-in-law. Even today the wife of an eldest son, like Bora, is expected to take his parents into her home in their old age, although younger women are pushing back against that custom.

Bora is only a few generations removed from the time when Korean *mat'sons* were arranged by a *jung-me* who studied the resumes of young men and women to find a compatible match of age, social status, blood lines, and astrological signs. Papers were exchanged and the lunar calendar consulted to determine compatibility between the families. Usually the couple did not meet until the day of the wedding. Marriage, after all, was not the result of love between two people, but rather the successful merger of two families. That may explain why the young women in my class were so in love with the idea of love.

"Tell me about your love story," Bora asked one day. When I told her we met in college and fell quickly in love, she sighed. "I wanted a fairy tale romance, too."

I suspect my grandparents, like many of their generation, would have preferred that their children marry within their culture, a way of staying connected to the countries they left behind. In a picture taken on my parents' wedding day, they stand on the steps of the church with my father's brother and my mother's sister, their attendants. My mother's aunt Edith stands behind them throwing rice. I once asked my mother if she had a picture of my grandparents on her wedding day. "Oh, nobody went to weddings in those days," she said, waving the question away with her hand. I somehow knew not to ask about the picture of my aunt standing on the altar with her parents. I think there were fewer Catholics than Protestants in Reliance when my parents were of marriageable age, so many wed someone who didn't share their heritage. Faith trumped ethnicity.

Bora interrupts my thoughts. "I don't like the man he is in Korea. I made him promise we can move back to Canada. Everything is better in the West."

"You lived in Canada, Bora? What were you doing there?"

She plops down in the chair and examines the clasp on her bracelet as if she'd never before seen the tiny butterfly dangling on its chain.

"My husband and I studied English there."

I want to ask her more about Canada, but she tucks her head into her shoulder like a baby chick hiding under its wing. So I drop the subject. When she jiggles her foot, the plastic blossoms on her sandals flash in the sunlight.

Flower-shaped earrings with rhinestone centers glittered on the mannequins in the Fantle's Department Store windows. Their marble eyes were vacant beneath wiry lashes and penciled eyebrows, as if they were bored with the work of luring customers into the store. They seemed indifferent to the teenage girl standing on the sidewalk who yearned to be as fashionable as they.

Fantle's sat on the corner of a busy intersection in Sioux Falls, the city on the eastern border of the state where my father sold his feeder cattle. It was an elegant building with pilasters and a metallic awning shaped like a half moon at the entrance and window displays that changed with the seasons. It was the place where I first navigated the geography of longing.

When I was small, I looked forward to the days we took our Herefords to market in Sioux Falls. The men in manure-caked boots and cowboy hats shouting "yup, yup, yup" as they waded through a sea of brown, the dust kicked up by the cattle's hooves, and the musty smell of cowhide. There was even mystery in the Stockmans' Café, where my father and oldest brother ate lunch along with other cattlemen, mysterious because Mother insisted the rest of us eat sandwiches in the car. Perhaps the sheer maleness of that café unsettled her.

But in my teenage years, I saw no romance in the markets—men hollering and cattle bellowing, smoke stacks from a nearby packing plant belching the odor of offal and blood. I only came to market day so that I could later stroll down Phillips Avenue through tall buildings, crowds, and stoplights, absent from my small town. Here I could study the mannequins' perky breasts, Kewpie doll lips, and wigs that framed their faces in stiff parentheses, and imagine myself wearing a slim skirt, cropped jacket, gloves, and kitten heels. I could almost feel the silky fur of mink draped around my neck. I practiced jutting my hip forward, my hand on my hip, looking bored.

I carefully planned my wardrobe for market days. Cutoff jeans and sweatshirt? Casual and outdoorsy. Cotton shirtdress with penny loafers? Classic. One year, I chose a turquoise dress with a black belt and lace-trimmed collar. As I stood at that window feeling very urban, clusters of girls with sun-bleached hair and plaid Bermuda shorts strolled by me. The tinkling of their charm bracelets was laughter at a country girl in her matronly dress and with dull pennies in her shoes. I felt myself disappearing. At the same time, I felt as if all eyes were on me.

But my family didn't shop at Fantles. We walked to Kresge's Five and Dime, where rows of fluorescent lights that hung from the ceiling failed to eliminate the cavernous feeling in a room that was crowded. The floor creaked as I walked past tables stacked with shoe boxes. There was the smell of cheap dye in the bins of underwear and socks. While I tugged at dresses and jackets bunched on racks like cattle in loading chutes, the salesclerk slouched over the cash register cracking her gum and staring out the window.

*   *   *

"Is it true that young Americans live together without being married?" Bora's eyes, beneath inky-black lashes, are narrowed as if she expects me to evade her question.

Bora is among several students who have come to my office for group conversation. The other students look up in surprise at her question. I suspect Bora would not ask this question of a Korean professor. I run my finger over the lip of my coffee cup while I consider how to answer her.

"Yes," I finally say, "many couples do share housing without being married." My answer takes the students into an intimate discussion that must make them uncomfortable, yet I can see they are curious.

"Korean parents would never allow that," Bora says. "They say we can't be, what is the right word, close before marriage?"

I don't know how to avoid answering her questions. "Do you mean sexually intimate?"

Bora digs through her Hello Kitty backpack for her notebook and pen. She holds the notebook close to her breasts as she scribbles something. I see a photo of a baby with spiky hair and chubby cheeks in a nest of hair ribbons at the bottom of her backpack. I decide not to ask about the picture. But I suspect it has something to do with her question.

She puts the notebook and pen away and thinks for a moment before saying, "We sneak out of the house to meet boys at DVD *bangs* so parents don't see us together."

Ken and I went to a DVD *bang* a few times, picked out a movie, and took it to a small room with a love seat, ottoman, and a large projection screen. One wall was polarized glass, and as we watched the movie, I always felt as if someone was looking at us through the glass. When I told the students that Ken and I had frequented the DVD *bangs*, they were shocked. "Why did you go there?" Bora asked. "That's for dating."

That's when I understood that because many Korean students live at home, the DVD *bangs* are one of the few places where young couples can be alone. It was sexual tension I felt in that small room. Now I was the voyeur standing on the other side of the glass, peering into my students' private space of longing and furtive fumbling.

Bora swivels back and forth in her chair for a moment before saying, "I gave my husband an *adeul*. It is right for the first child to be a boy. Now everybody must pay attention to me because I am the mother of a son."

137

There is silence. We are all caught off guard by this confession. Finally, Luke, the party boy with chiseled arms and an impish grin, says, "You're too young to be married and have a baby. You aren't supposed to do that until you're out of college."

She glares at him. "Well I am married and I have my son. He was born in Canada."

"Why did you have your baby in Canada?" Honey objects. "You should have had the baby in Korea so your mother could help."

Bora ignores the question. Conversations with Bora were like the time I poured hot water over a jasmine pod at the bottom of my goblet in a Chinese restaurant. The lavender petals unfolded one layer at a time until a fully-blossomed flower floated in the water, its rich floral fragrance scenting the table. But the taste of the tea was bitter.

I am certain now that she and her husband did not go to Canada to study English but were sent away until a baby was born. In high school, I knew a few pregnant and unmarried girls who lived with family in other towns or in homes for unwed mothers during their pregnancy. Many came back with stories of vague illnesses. Did Bora and her husband return home with a story of a premature birth and strangely healthy birth weight?

When I was a sophomore in high school, a friend told me she was pregnant and getting married. I was shocked. I didn't know that girls my age had sex, although I later realized many did but wouldn't admit it to a virgin like me. I was filling my car at the gas station after a basketball game the night of their wedding. My friend had been a cheerleader until she had to turn in the pleated skirt and the bulky sweater with a school letter stitched to it. It was snowing hard, and I didn't see their car until it pulled up to the pump next to me. The boy got out. His sports coat was thin, and he shivered in the wind, but I remember mostly how pale and somehow exposed his scalp seemed beneath his dark crew cut. As I leaned in the window to talk to her, I could smell the carnations in her corsage. Snow glistened on her cheeks, and her wide-set eyes like Jackie Kennedy's were checkered behind a chin-length veil.

She had longed to date this senior boy, the charmer with the long eyelashes, had plotted ways to be near him in the school halls. She'd left me alone at the movies while she necked with him in the back row, and crept out her

138

bedroom window to meet him on the river bank. I envied her when they started dating. I wondered if she was thrilled to get what she had so desperately wanted. She waved as they drove away. "We're headed to the Black Hills for our honeymoon. I'll call you when we get back." I watched their car cross the river until the taillights were snuffed out by horizontal sheets of snow.

After my friend returned from their honeymoon, they moved into his parents' basement. He was allowed to attend classes at the high school, but she had to take correspondence lessons at home. Like Bora sequestered in a foreign country to hide her swollen belly, my friend was caged in concrete blocks and narrow windows to hide her shame.

When I visited her, she was alone in the basement while his mother watched television upstairs, some game show with screaming women and catchy music. There was a washing machine and furnace in one corner of the room. In another, golf clubs, shelves of tools, and packing boxes. T-shirts and underwear dried on a wooden rack under the transom window.

They hung sheets from the ceiling to delineate the living room and bedroom. When I saw the bed I felt excited and curious, but squeamish at the thought of the desperate fumbling that led to that bump in her belly. A rack of clothes hung above the bed. She pulled a dress from the rack. "I bought this to wear to the Sadie Hawkins Dance. It doesn't fit me now. Of course I couldn't go anyway. But that's okay. I married the man I loved." Did she hear the past tense in that verb?

I didn't see much of her after that day. I couldn't face that basement cell again, and she rarely left the house. Now I can't recall if the walls of sheets were patterned or solid-colored. I don't remember anything about the dress. Did it have sequins on the bodice and ruffles on the skirt? Was there really a television blaring upstairs and underwear drying on a rack? Did she really say "loved?" Or did I invent these details because her life seemed so bleak to me? I do, however, clearly recall the yellow layette set on a folding chair, the bulge in her tummy, and the sliver of sky in the transom windows.

When I was a freshman at South Dakota State University, I finally walked through the doors to Fantles' Department Store into a new world of Bobbie Brooks dresses and Mary Quant miniskirts. I plopped berets on my hair and tilted them to a perky angle, ran my fingers over leather purses, and stroked the wool of sherbet-colored cardigans. A clerk scurried about sliding coats off racks and holding them as I slipped my arms through the sleeves. I could smell My Sin perfume on her wrists as she adjusted the collar and patted the shoulder pads into place. When I twirled in front of the mirror, she sighed. "You look so sophisticated in that coat." So of course I bought it, a gray Chesterfield with a black velvet collar, as well as leather gloves, a watermelon-pink cardigan, and Bonnie Doone anklets, luxuries my father with two children in college probably could not afford.

It was my first shopping trip to Sioux Falls with my freshman roommate, a debutante who arrived at campus after a graduation trip abroad. She flounced into our room hauling red Samsonite luggage, the pricey set I had admired in *Seventeen Magazine.* She gave me a hug and plopped on her bed. I smoked my first cigarette that night, choking on the smoke that curled down my throat. Still, I held the cigarette between my fingers, feeling like Holly Golightly, a woman of savoir faire—a word my roommate used. We talked until late at night. She spoke easily of Jean Valjean and Madame Bovary, Paris and the Louvre, as I spoke of Sue Barton and Nancy Drew, the Badlands and the Corn Palace. When it was time to sleep, she knelt by the bed, rosary in hand, and prayed, *"Je vous salue, Marie, pleine de grâce."*

The next day, we went to the student union. She dragged me from booth to booth to meet other girls and waved gaily at boys in football jerseys playing pool across the room. Their eyes followed her as she walked away. I was a little in love with her, the way awkward girls often are when someone confident and attractive lets us stand in her light.

We left Fantles and walked down Phillips Avenue to Lemonds Restaurant. I held my bag so that the Fantles' logo could be seen. The restaurant was Art Deco style with gold-trimmed sconces in each booth and metallic chandeliers. Jazz played in the background, Duke Ellington, or maybe Glenn Miller. The fragrance of sweetheart roses in crystal vases mingled with the smell of bleach on white linens. A waiter in a tuxedo shirt brought us baskets of sweet buns and Parker House rolls, and as I recall, chilled plates with pats of butter bearing the letter L. We ordered chicken à la king in pastry cups. How optimistic, or pathetic, was I to serve that same meal at my wedding four years later.

In November, I took my roommate home on a weekend. We clung to the tailgate of the truck as my father zigged and zagged through a pasture. My cotton socks from Sears catalog were gray with dust. Beneath the smell of gasoline fumes was the odor of manure and musty cattle. There was a hollow where the grass was trampled bare by cattle, except for a few patches of green still pushing up through the sod. At that spot, a wild-eyed steer mounted an impassive heifer. "What's that cow doing?" she asked. When I explained about steers and bulls and heifers in heat, she gasped and her eyes widened. Then she laughed so hard I had to grab her arm to keep her from falling out of the truck. "This is so fun," she said. Our friendship seemed as promising as those shoots of grass. It would be my road map to a world I would explore with savoir-faire.

That night, my family gathered around the Formica table in a knotty pine paneled room, a freezer against one wall and piles of boots and sneakers in the corner. The floral oilcloth shone garishly in the fluorescent lights. In the way of large families, we laughed often and loudly, each of us vying for attention. Mother broiled t-bone steaks—rare and juicy, and so flavorful that only a sprinkle of salt was needed—as well as baked potatoes, celery ribs stuffed with peanut butter, and apple pie. We ate off melmac plates and drank milk from jelly glasses.

Although I was proud of my family's bantering, my father's cattle, and the steaks my mother broiled, I couldn't help wondering who I would be if my father wielded a golf club instead of a branding iron and my mother's hands were covered in jewels, not flour. I couldn't help wondering what it would feel like to be a girl in a white dress descending a staircase in a country club with everyone's eyes on me.

At our last conference, Bora stands at my office door holding something behind her back. She is shy but excited as she hands me a box wrapped in *hanji* and tied with a raffia ribbon. "I gave this *seonmul*, what you would call a gift, to the guests at my son's *doljanchi*, his first birthday party. Now you will not forget me when you are home in America."

Inside the box are tea cups etched with pictures of wood violets and these words: *I think I grow tension/ Like flowers/ In a wood where/ Nobody goes.*

I am puzzled at the poem. Her English seems too rudimentary to understand the complexities beneath the simple words. Then again, the haiku comes out of a rich Asian literary tradition; perhaps she grasped their meaning. But why give these cups as gifts for her son's birthday party? What was she trying to say, if anything?

"Bora, do you still want to move to Canada some day?"

"Of course, but it is not possible." She doesn't look at me.

"How do you feel about this?"

"I don't like it," she shrugs her shoulders, "but what can I do? It is the way it is."

She shows me a picture of the rosy-cheeked baby dressed in *dol-bok*. The tunic and pants are snug against his chubby body. He sits on a table next to a photo of Samshin, incense and candles flickering in front of her. "We give thanks to the birth goddess for our son," she says. "She answered our prayers." Her voice seems wistful.

"Korea is a good place to raise my boy. The Confucian culture treats men with honor."

When she leaves my office, the room seems darker somehow.

Everything glittered that night—chandeliers, gold threads running through the ivory brocade that swooped across the windows, oil paintings of ocean waves crashing against rocks. Creamy damask covered the table and calla lilies in crystal vases perfumed the room. My roommate's father and mother sat at opposite ends of a table. I always imagine her mother in a sheath with pearls, he in suit and tie, and my pink cardigan turning coral in the candlelight. I explored a new terrain of tableware—sterling fruit spoons, salad forks, and butter knives; bone china trimmed in green and gold; crystal goblets with slices of lemon on the rims. I watched the mother and made mental notations of when and how she used the silverware.

A woman served us squares of rye bread covered with a creamy paste called pâté. There was Cornish hen stuffed with rice and pecans, and asparagus spears with a white sauce I later learned was hollandaise. For dessert, chocolate pudding, or mousse as my roommate called it, served in a crystal dish. Her younger brothers and sisters ate in the kitchen, and our conversation was so quiet, I swear I heard the needle running through the grooves playing Chopin. Perhaps I invent some of these details, but that night was so far beyond my own experience that exaggeration still seems impossible.

After supper, we went into the living room, where a grand piano sat in front of a bay window overlooking a park. In the glow of street lights, the leaves on the maple trees were sparklers on the Fourth of July as if celebrating the birth of my new country. Her parents knew I had studied piano, and they asked me to play for them. I chose "Fur Elise" and "Moonlight Sonata" for the maximum of splash with the minimum of skill. They praised me and asked about my favorite composers. I was proud that I could explain the expressive music of Chopin and compare it to the Baroque structure of Bach compositions.

They said they wished to speak to their daughter in private. I went into the library with plush chairs, lamps with cut-glass bases, and a hide-a-bed made up with freshly-ironed sheets and down pillows. I put on my new coat and studied myself in a mirror as I remembered every detail of the night. China, sterling silver, crystal, and pearls were the legend on the map I was drawing for myself.

Then I overheard her father say, "You could attend a convent school in France, improve your French, take classes on French Impressionists. A private education would help you grow intellectually."

I thought I heard her mother say, "You need more culture and the opportunity to be with sophisticated people."

In the mirror I saw myself eating dinner off mish-mash dinnerware. I smelled the heat of animals. Even the coat now seemed cheap on me. One day, I will eat foie gras on a triangle of toast, and drink champagne in Paris. I will learn the difference between Manet and Monet, between an oyster fork and dessert fork. But I didn't know that then, nor did I know that by time I traveled to France I would prefer jeans to pencil skirts and flannel to fur.

Now I am convinced it was my insecurities, not my friend and her parents, who made me feel inferior. Her parents were kind to me that night and invited me to spend more weekends with them. But I knew they were sending her to Europe to get away from a girl like me who knew more about sex-crazed steers and heifers in heat than she did Monet and foie gras. I crawled into bed, turned off the light, and lifted my hands in front of my face. They disappeared in the dark.

Chapter Fourteen

A tiny boy in a pressed white shirt buttoned at the neck and khaki pants with crisp creases clutches the microphone stand, his hands shaking. He speaks so softly I lean forward to better hear him. He struggles to pronounce the words. Articles are lost in a jumble of nouns, and verb tenses are colts skittering between sentences. In a dingy auditorium, he speaks of the sun shining on a garden and of his grandmother scratching at the dirt with her rake, teaching him about seeds and saplings, hoeing and harvesting.

"I have worries," he says, "because grandmother have no husband. She live alone." But she tells him that as long as she can work in her garden, she will never be lonely, and he is not to worry about her. He says he will always remember his grandmother bending over her vegetables. "I never forget forever smell of dirt under her nails."

He bows and shuffles off the stage, shoulders slumped.

I am judging the Daejeon Middle School English Speaking Contest. The teacher and the student who wins the competition bring honor to the school, so principals and administrators from the Central Education Office have come to hear fifty children give stilted, grammatically perfect speeches I suspect were written by parents—like the text a CNU professor asked me to record for his daughter. He said she didn't have time to come to visit with me. "She has too much schoolwork."

He held the microphone to my mouth. "Stop," he said often. "Can you repeat that word more slowly so she hears your accent? She needs to have perfect English so she wins this contest."

I squirmed, thinking this recording would give his daughter an unfair advantage. Then I learned she would be competing in the more challenging division for children who have lived in English-speaking countries. I admit to feeling guilty relief when she didn't place.

The pressure to excel is evident. The boys stare at the floor, speak in a monotone, and bolt from the stage when

144

their talks are over. The girls look at the ceiling, fidget with their hair, and shuffle their feet. One girl talks about the World Baseball Classic, praising Korea's team for competing so well against the "arrogant Japanese" and the "unfair Americans." When she takes her bow, she sees me at the judges' table and races off the stage, a look of horror on her face.

I had agreed to be a judge as a favor to a colleague. By the end of the day, I'm weary from listening to children regurgitate memorized speeches I suspect were written by their parents. The children look rumpled and relieved as well that the day is over. When the superintendent announces the gold medal winner, a small girl covers her face and sobs while her teacher pats her back and whispers to her. I am unnerved by her tears. What do I accomplish by teaching English in another country? What message do I give these children about their own language?

The director of the competition approaches me and says, "Thank you for doing this. Seeing a Westerner at the table made the students work harder to speak perfect English, which prepares them for success." I smile, but some unhappy memory tugs at me. I look for the little boy who spoke of his grandmother in the garden. I want to tell him that I thought his speech was wonderful. But he has disappeared. I walk up the aisle through the smell of must and disappointment and step outside where the sun breaks through the clouds.

Every fall when I was growing up, yellow buses, bright as sunshine, rumbled into my hometown delivering children from the nearby reservations to the Indian boarding school on the Missouri River bluffs. Their arrival was as reliable as the migration of geese over the river and just as mysterious. What brought the children back every year? Why did I never see them at the movies or the swimming pool? Where were their parents?

There were stories about their first day at the school. Of children standing in tubs naked and shivering as nuns with sleeves rolled up to their elbows scrubbed their bare skin raw, of hair doused with lye then chopped straight and level below their ears like the little boy on paint cans in our garage. Clothes the children wore to school were burned, and they were issued garments donated by rich people from the East Coast, clothes too big and old fashioned for school kids.

I knew little else about them, except that they would not go home for nine months. My stomach gnawed at the thought of how homesick they would be in nights to come, lying in rows of cots, their sniffling layered beneath the silence. Still, I believed taking them away from the reservation was necessary. Years later I would learn that the Lakota believe hair contains the soul and is to be cut only with great ceremony, that the Lakota word for child, *cinca*, translates to "standing sacred." The boarding school believed their mission was sacred—killing the Indian to save the man. I didn't question that mission.

I rarely saw the Indian children after the buses arrived. Occasionally the priest took my Catechism class to the campus for Friday night roller skating in a gymnasium lit by bare bulbs hanging in wire cages from the ceiling. I had never been to a roller skating rink, but I had seen pictures of a ball of mirrors rotating above the floor in a rink in California. The mirrors scattered pixie dust over the room as lovers held hands and twirled around the floor. But there was no magic in the swirls of dust that rose beneath the wheels of our skates and no hand-holding under the watchful eye of Father John.

My friends and I rolled in one direction—usually in the middle of the room—while the Indian children skated in the opposite direction, hugging the wall. I said "Hi" or "How are you?" the first time I skated past them. They mumbled something, perhaps in English, maybe Lakota. After that first greeting, I made no attempt to bridge whatever language gap existed between us. All night long, I spun past them, gliding on skates to organ music coming from a record player.

When I enter the classroom for the first English conversation class, students leap from their desks, snap their feet together, and bow. I print my name on the board and turn to the students saying "*Aneyong haseyeo.*" They stare at me, eyes crinkled with puzzlement. I say it again, putting more emphasis on "*ha.*" I laugh when a young man asks, "Are you saying hello?"

"Yes, but apparently not well."

I consult my dictionary of Korean phrases so I can ask them to introduce themselves. "*Insahaseyo,*" I say. The students look confused again. I hand the book to a young man and point to the phrase: "What is your name?"

"Aaaah." He interprets for the students. They look relieved to understand what I want.

Then each student stands up and bows. "*Chei·reum·eun*, my name is Honey." "*Chei·reum·eun*, my name is Gil."

In the way that Indian children were forbidden to keep their Lakota names or to speak their native tongue at the boarding schools, Koreans were assigned Japanese names during the occupation in the early twentieth century and Japanese was taught in the schools. Elderly Koreans still suffer a feeling of disconnectedness because they were forced to speak another language.

When Indian children were denied their language— "the devils tongue," they were told—they also felt disconnected. *Mitakuye oyasin*, which means "all my relatives," is a phrase that expresses the Native American belief that all forms of life are interconnected. This connection is embedded in much of the vocabulary of the Lakota, and so it offers the security of place to those who speak it. For native children, losing their language must have deepened their sense of isolation.

Many Korean students now voluntarily choose English names when they study the language. "It's good for us to use English names instead of Korean names," Gil says. "It's very difficult for Westerners to pronounce Korean words."

But some of my students have kept their Korean names, and my Western tongue struggles to unravel the letters so I can pronounce Hyun·jun, Seo·jeon, Ye·eun. They patiently repeat their names for me, sympathetic to my stumbling over the vowels and syllables. I am both relieved when I don't have to struggle to use Hangul names in front of my students and ashamed at how quickly I accept my students using English names for my convenience.

One day, Gil says, "English is the most important language in the world. If we want to succeed we must master the pronunciation."

Perhaps that is why some Korean parents ask doctors to perform a frenectomy on their children, a procedure that clips a band of tissue under the tongue. This surgery supposedly lengthens the tongue and makes it more flexible to handle the letters "l" and "r." Even if the surgery achieves what it promises, what damage has been done to those tiny mouths? To their pride in being Korean?

The emphasis on speaking perfect English has caused many young Koreans to be so fearful of making mistakes that they refused to talk to us. One day, as Ken and I walked up to the ticket booth at the Daejeon Cultural Center, the young woman selling tickets saw us, hopped off her stool, and ran out of the booth. We waited for several minutes before a young man, his face flushed, came out of the back room. "She is ashamed that her English is bad."

There is shame, too, in skating past Lakota children in a dusty gymnasium and not noticing their dark eyes dull with homesickness, in being ignorant of dark closets and lashes against bare skin. There is shame in assuming that Indian children must be more like me.

"You seem like an intelligent woman. What do you think about the emphasis Koreans place on learning English?"

I am a guest speaker at the CNU English Club, which has the mission of preparing students for the Test of English Competency, a standardized exam that focuses on conversational and business English. The club meets weekly to read and discuss articles in *Time Magazine,* a daunting and frustrating task for the members who struggle to read the simplest English. Yet they soldier on, knowing a high score on the exam is a condition for employment with many Korean companies.

I have just finished my talk about reading strategies when a man with black glasses and hair shiny with butch wax and combed neatly to the side stands up, bows, and asks me this question.

Before I can answer, he says, "I understand employees in Korean companies who work directly with Americans should speak fluent English. But why," he holds out his hands, palms up, "why should a company like Hyundai expect an accountant to speak English? Why should job interviews in Korea be conducted in English?"

The club members shift in their chairs and look at each other with nervous eyes.

"It's ridiculous," he says. "English language institutes are cash cows making money off Koreans."

I am both impressed with his use of "cash cow" and troubled by his comments.

In a shaky voice, the club president declares the meeting over. The young man bows and leaves the room.

We troop down the hill to a pub in Gung Dong where we sip *maekju* and snack on sushi, strips of dried squid, and roasted peanuts.

"*Choe-song-ham-ni-da,*" a woman apologizes, wiping foam from the lip of her mug. "It is not right for him to shame a foreigner."

Although the young man had embarrassed the club members by infiltrating their meeting, he raised valid questions, questions that I had begun to ask myself about teaching English in another country. I thought of his words as he left the meeting. "Korea is an ancient and honorable country. If we lose our language, we lose our culture."

I parked on a wide bluff overlooking the river and turned off the engine. It was Christmas Eve, the year I got my driver's license, and I had begged my parents to let me take a drive during the hours between gift opening and midnight mass. I drove north down Main Street toward the boarding school, a place I loved for its silence and the wide view of the river. As I remember, mine was the only car on Main Street, except for a rusty pickup parked outside the saloon where a lone man sat at the bar, his face blurred by smoke and the frost on the windows. On the radio Frank Sinatra sang "Have yourself a Merry little Christmas, let your heart be light." The glow from Christmas lights strung between street lamps turned the snowflakes into starbursts as if I were driving inside the Milky Way.

At the end of Main, I turned into the school's entrance and drove past dormitories to a parking lot on the bluffs. I rolled down the window. The smell of pines mingled with the fragrances of tomatoes and fried onions. It came from a basement kitchen where nuns scurried from counters to stoves, their black veils fluttering like crows swooping down on crickets.

The air was still and the snow swirled around the car, silent as confetti. I stuck my hand out the window, watched snowflakes collect on my palm, then licked them off my skin until my tongue tingled. I was satiated with the gifts of sweaters and anklets, Black Hills gold jewelry and books, oyster stew and ribbon candy. In the moonlight, the frozen river and the clear sky were so luminous that night might have been day and time seemed suspended. For that moment, I believed I would always be sixteen, always this happy, and life would always be a car ride through a shower of confetti.

In the rear view mirror, I saw a nun wrapped in a black cape, her veil floating behind her as she strode down the sidewalk toward the red glow of a sanctuary lamp shining through stained glass. A string of girls followed her. Their hair was short and they wore old-lady shoes with laces and coats so long the hems brushed the snow. I felt sorry for

149

the girls and grateful that my own blonde hair fell to my waist and my clothes were youthful.

The nun opened the door to the chapel and tapped each girl on the head as she walked by. I remembered stories of runaways and realized she was probably counting to make sure no girl had slipped away in the dark. I had a vision of a young girl running up the bluff and hiding in the scrubby shrubs covered with snow, imagined her looking to the night sky to find her way home. The snow was still falling when I drove back down Main, but the Christmas lights were no longer stars shimmering in the sky, but simply cheap bulbs on strings of wire.

"I am staying in America," fourteen-year-old Janie Park announced, her black eyes flashing. "I need to learn English so I can get into a very important college and then have a good career."

Mrs. Park, a slight woman with smooth skin and delicate features, put down her fork and gripped my arm. Her eyes filled with tears. She spoke little English, but she understood this argument. She shook her head, "*Neh*, too young."

We met the Park family during our time in Korea. They often included us in dinner parties at Korean restaurants and picnics with friends in a park along the river. Dr. Park came the next year to SDSU as an exchange professor. His wife and daughter accompanied him. I prepared a South Dakota feast of baked pheasant, scalloped corn, coleslaw, and apple pie.

The Korean government estimates more than two hundred thousand Korean students live in English-speaking countries at a cost of four billion dollars a year. Some mothers even move to America with their children to enroll them in high schools in hopes it will improve their English and their chances of being admitted to prestigious American universities. The fathers stay in Korea.

"They are called goose fathers," Dr. Park said, "because like geese they migrate between America and Korea. Many fathers see their children only in the summers."

The next year, Janie returned to South Dakota to live with a host family in Sioux Falls. Four years later, when they attended her high school graduation, they were shocked by the changes in her. Burgundy streaks in her hair, tight t-shirt, and low-slung jeans. When she bent over, I glimpsed a flower tattoo on her lower back. She also had a steady boyfriend, a secret she kept from her parents for over a year. Her parents spoke to her in Korean. She answered in English, often using slang they didn't under-stand. "She is too American now," Mr. Park said.

The Parks insisted that Janie return to Korea with them to attend the university. But she refused and enrolled at the same public university that her boyfriend attended. Her parents went home. We have not heard from them since.

Hoping to ease the financial and personal burdens for Korean families like the Parks, the government has constructed a ninety million dollar, English-only theme park called Paju on a long-vacant piece of land near the DMZ. Paju is a replica of an English village, which can accom-modate seven hundred students—some as young as seven. Tuition per child is approximately forty-five hundred dollars for three days.

One hundred and fifty native speakers live and teach in Paju, joining more than seven thousand other Western-ers who—like me—have come to each English in this coun-try called the Republic of Tutors. They patrol the village walking by a miniature Buckingham Palace, ivy-covered pubs, red telephone booths, and signs that read in English "landmines nearby." They issue demerit points to students caught speaking Korean. The cycle of punishment for using their language once imposed on their great grandparents continues, although now voluntarily. Will these children remember these days with the same bitterness?

Whenever I return to my hometown, I visit the boarding school on the river. Much of what I loved about the campus is the same today as when I was young—the old trees spreading their branches over the sidewalks, the spacious lawns, the grassy bluffs, and the breathtaking view of the river.

But much has changed as well. Yellow buses no longer bring children to the school. Parents or grandparents apply for the children's admission. The younger students live in apartments with house parents while teenagers live in the community and attend my old high school. Children can visit their families whenever they like.

Lakota language is taught as well as Lakota legends and myths, the stories of chiefs and elders, and the events that shaped Lakota history. There is a powwow on the river bluffs every fall where the children dance the jingle dress dance, the fancy dance, the grass dance. The beads and feathers on their ceremonial garments are whirlwinds of colors flashing in the sun as if a painting by Oscar Howe, a Lakota artist with international fame, had come to life.

The stained glass windows in Our Lady of the Sioux Chapel depict Lakota rites—*hunkapi*, the making of relatives; *wiwanyag wachipi*, the sundance; and *nagi gluhapi*, the keeping of the soul. In an alcove near the altar, the Blessed Virgin holds the child, her hair in long braids, his hair held back with a beaded headband. Both wear buckskin and feathers. On the back wall above the altar is a floor-to-ceiling weaving of a Lakota warrior hanging on the cross beneath a midnight-blue sky. A white cyclone swirls around him as if the whole earth were roiling at his sacrifice.

The Akta Lakota Museum (the name means Honor the People) houses several interactive exhibits that explain the culture and the history of the Lakota. An art gallery displays oil paintings and watercolors, ceramics and beadwork, and sculptures of alabaster and bronze, many done by former students.

Tokeya unki najinpi (We Stood Here in the Beginning) is a new wing with a hands-on exhibit for children that teaches the history of the school. I took my six-year-old grandson, Casey, to the museum, where he pretended to eat from tin plates on a wooden table, tried on children's jackets and hats, and studied a photo on the wall of somber-eyed children in denim and gingham sitting on benches in front of a dormitory.

How often has Casey flashed a big, goofy grin to please me when I take his picture? "Say cheese, Casey." But the children at the boarding school had no grandma to coax them into smiling.

When Casey stepped into a replica of a yellow bus and sat on a bench, his brown eyes shining at the imaginary journey, memories of other children unfolded. I saw dark eyes, framed by the windows of another bus, staring at a blue-eyed girl who would go home to her family that night and fall asleep to her mother playing the piano and to her father singing "Just Molly and me, and baby makes three. We're happy in my blue Heaven."

A Native American girl, about ten years old, bent over her desk and read from her journal. Her boots were dusty and her jeans faded, but her black hair glistened in the sunlight. I was spending the day at a small elementary school in the middle of one of the largest mixed-grass prairies in the United States. The children came from ranches, reservations, the small town, and from the Badlands National Park, where their families worked and lived.

To the north were the smoky-gray mesas in the park where I lived for five weeks in the fall of 2008 as an artist in residence. The morning sun cast light and shadows over the mesas and tinged the fossilized soils running through clay in rose-colored bands. I read some poems about the land and gave them exercises that focused on sensory imagery. I asked them to write a poem or short paragraph describing the land where they lived. "What do you want me to know about where you live?" They wrote in the language of their place—of blue grama, buffalo grass, prickly pear, and blazing star; of antelope and bighorn sheep, bobcats and bison.

The little girl read of prairie violets nestled in the grass around her house and of *pispisaz* popping their rodent faces from mounds of dirt in the prairie. She wrote of the smell of hair and flesh on her *sunkawakan* when she pressed her face against its flanks and the sound of hay crunching as the horse shifted against her. She read in a quiet voice, and the children listened, resting their chins on their hands, their faces dreamy. I heard the voice of a shy little boy whose meticulous attention to the smell of dirt under an old woman's fingernails took us into his grandmother's garden the way this girl's words invited us into her world. For that moment, there was only the smell of sage drifting through the window, the chattering of a magpie from a tree, and a sky of shifting colors—robin's egg blue, cornflower blue, teal blue.

CHAPTER FIFTEEN

On a winter evening in South Korea, I sit in Dr. Nho's silent apartment while the spirit of a dead woman eats her meal at a table a few feet away.

Growing up near the Lower Brule and the Crow Creek reservations, I heard stories about Native Americans eating meals on family graves. Picnics in cemeteries seemed spooky and dangerously pagan for a little Catholic girl, although I didn't know what the word pagan meant or how much pagan traditions had influenced my own religion. Nor did I know that I would turn to the rituals of ancient cultures to help me finally grieve my father's death and to mourn my mother's recent passing.

August 22, 1968, just two months to the day I married Ken, I watched my father's copper-colored casket lowered into the grave, incense curling around it, the ground softly acquiescing to its weight.

"Eternal rest grant unto him, O Lord, and let the perpetual light shine upon him," the priest prayed as he sprinkled holy water over the casket and the withered grass.

"May his soul and all the souls of the faithful departed rest in peace." I mumbled the response but I didn't really hear the words.

The spring of 1968 was a season of loss for me. On April 4, I was student teaching at a junior high in Watertown, an hour away from the SDSU campus. It was the end of the day, and I was sipping a beer with other student teachers in the Office Bar when Walter Cronkite appeared on the television to report that Martin Luther King Jr. had been assassinated. I watched, stunned, as the events unfolded on the television—his body lying on a balcony at the Lorraine Motel in Memphis, his aides kneeling around him. People wept in the streets, and Coretta Scott King sat in her pew at Ebenezer Baptist Church, dazed and stoic.

Two months later, I watched news clips of Robert Kennedy sprawled on a corridor floor in the Ambassador

Hotel. Ethel bent over him, her hands cupped as if whispering something to him. Across the room, my father leaned back in his recliner, thin and tired and complaining of stomach pains. When the train that carried Senator Kennedy's body from New York City to Washington, D.C., arrived at Union Station, I was certain it marked the end of the spring of death and violence that defined my twenty-second year. Two weeks later, my father was diagnosed with stomach cancer.

In the days after my father's funeral, I served coffee and cake to friends and family who stopped by the house. We talked about everything but his dying. Many told anecdotes about my father. "I never knew anyone that could use a blow torch with such skill. He was an artist at welding," said one neighbor.

"Did you know that once the bishop stopped mass and turned around to watch your dad while he sang?" my father's good friend asked. "Then the bishop said, 'That is a voice from Heaven.'"

I craved those stories. At the same time, I wanted to tell someone that, with my father's death, I knew my world would never feel safe again. But I couldn't speak those words. I felt no one wanted to hear them. Instead my aunts and uncles encouraged me to focus on the future and remember that my father would want me to be happy. "He wouldn't want you to be sad," they said. They didn't understand that I was numb. I didn't cry during the rosary service or at the funeral. Or even when I said goodbye to Mother. I went back to work a few days later and rarely spoke of my father's death.

For twenty years after my father died, I had a recurring dream that I was driving the gravel road that led to our farm. I turn east at the cemetery where the graves of my Catholic ancestors are separated from the Protestants by an invisible, inviolable line. Crumbling stones and cedar trees stunted by drought are scattered through the cemetery. Farther down the road is the muddy Reliance Dam, where my father took us fishing on Sunday afternoons, baiting our hooks with earthworms and snapping bobbers on the lines. Then I drive past the south field, where I took bologna sandwiches, lemonade, and spice cake to my father, the two of us resting in the shade of the tractor tire while he ate.

When I make the final turn north to our place, fog rolls out of the ditches and envelopes the car. I get out and stand in the middle of the road, weeping. I know that on the other side of the haze is the farmhouse with pink hollyhocks growing to the bottoms of the windows. I can smell the musk of cattle as they move toward the feed troughs, and hear the hayloft's door banging in the wind. My father stands in the pasture, sheltering his eyes from the sun as he watches for the whirlwind of dust raised by my car. But I can't part the haze. I can't go home. I wake up from this dream, my face damp, my heart pounding.

The Lakota honor their dead by observing *Nagi Gluhapi*, the keeping of the soul ritual, which includes purifying a lock of the deceased's hair with smoke from sweet grass and placing the lock in a buckskin pouch. At the end of the year, the bundle is carried outside and opened to release the soul. I bundled up my grief like a lock of hair and put it away, intending never to open it.

During our time in Korea, Dr. Nho was eager to share his culture with us. He took us to the baths, to a traditional music museum, and to a performance that combined traditional folk music and modern dance. Ancestor veneration ceremonies are essential to filial piety, a cornerstone of Confucian tradition. Only men can perform the ceremonies, and their faithfulness in continuing the traditions defines their worth as sons. As the eldest son, Dr. Nho is responsible for conducting the service. I am surprised and touched by his generosity in letting us witness this private family moment.

Against one wall in Dr. Nho's apartment is a linen screen stamped with images of men and women wearing *hanbok*. Pinned to the screen is the ancestor tablet. I study the characters on the paper, recalling the *Book of Remembrances* that lay on a stand in the vestibule at Saint Mary's. On All Souls' Day, I wrote my grandparents' names in the book so that Father would remember them during mass, his prayers freeing their souls from purgatory so they could at last enter Heaven. Because my grandparents died before I could retain them in memory, the act of writing their names in the book witnessed their existence for me and established my place in the lineage of the Woster and McManus families. Now, my parents' names are written in that book.

Shortly after Ken and I arrive at Dr. Nho's apartment, his brothers and their wives walk into the room carrying boxes with oxblood-red wooden pedestals, platters, and candlesticks. The women are friendly, but the men seem curt when we are introduced to them. Perhaps they don't speak English well. Maybe they resent our intrusion into this private moment. But I suspect they won't complain to Dr. Nho, for in Confucian custom, younger siblings must defer to the eldest son's wishes.

I go into the kitchen, where the women dust the serving pieces with paper towels and stretch plastic film over them. "It is not traditional to cover the pieces with Saran Wrap before putting food on them," one woman says, "but this way the dishes stay clean, and I won't have to wash them later. It will be late when we get back to Seoul, and I have to teach in the morning."

Two blood-red ceremonial tables are placed against the wall. On the smaller table are two long-handled soup spoons, chopsticks, a ceramic bowl with incense sticks stuck in raw rice, and candlesticks. On the ancestor table are candles, incense in a celadon bowl, and a photo of his mother, a chunky woman with a ribbon tied under the collar of her blouse. Her hair sweeps away from her face to expose a wide forehead and thick eyebrows. She looks back at her sons with pride. I admire and envy this table, with its tangible tribute to family heritage. Today in my home is a sofa table with votive candles, photos of our parents, and a small bundle of sage in a vase of Irish crystal.

The women come into the living room with platters of food. They arrange them on a table in a proscribed pattern of five rows: red foods—meat, apples, candies—on the east side and white foods—rice and pears—on the west. Across the bottom are dates, chestnuts, peaches, persimmons, grilled beef, dried sliced fish, and a grilled yellow fish, its head facing east for good luck and eternal life. They count the bowls, rearrange a few, and then tiptoe out of the room. As I listen to their whispering in the kitchen, I wonder if they are retelling stories of their mother-in-law. Or if they are complaining that the work of preparing the meal falls to them as it has for generations of women.

That quiet apartment sparks memories of my mother, strands of damp hair slipping out from under her hairnet and a flour sack apron covering her best dress. She peels potatoes and passes them to a woman who slices and layers them in large metal pans, while another woman adds chunks of ham and slathers the layers with cream sauce. Across the room, women giggle and gossip as they chop cabbage and carrots for coleslaw, butter the dinner rolls, and slice angel food and spice cakes.

Mother hauls a blue-speckled coffee pot to the cistern behind the church hall with sun-curdled siding at the end of Main Street. She sets it on a concrete slab beneath the spout and pumps the handle until water gurgles to the surface and flows into the pot. She lugs the pot back to the kitchen, hands wrapped around the wire handle. The kettle bounces against her thighs and sloshes water on her dress. She hoists the pot to the counter, measures coffee, stirs the grounds into the pot, and sets it over the flames of the coal-black range. When the water boils, she drops an egg into the pot and watches the swirls of yellow and white settle the grounds on the bottom. For me, a funeral ritual will always be the laughter of women, the taste of potatoes and ham, and the smell of coffee rising in steam from a blue-speckled coffee pot.

Dr. Nho opens the apartment door for his mother and pours a cup of rice wine into a bowl to serve the underground gods. He fills his mother's cup with wine to welcome her to the table. His brothers stand behind him as he kneels and lights the incense sticks. He touches his forehead to the floor, rises, and reads a short prayer on parchment paper. His brothers do the same.

He dips a spoon into a bowl of cooked rice, lays chopsticks over a plate of meat, and pulls the linen screen around the table so his mother can eat undisturbed. The men sit cross-legged on the floor, eyes closed, hands resting on their knees, thumbs and index fingers pinched together. The room smells of incense and fish frying in oil. Except for the crackling of candles and the sizzling of grease in a pan, the apartment is silent for five, maybe ten, minutes. Then Dr. Nho pulls back the screen, scoops a spoonful of rice into a bowl of water, and offers the rice water to his mother as a farewell gesture.

The *gi* ends when the men bow before their mother's photo, and Dr. Nho burns the ancestral tablet and the prayer on parchment. The women clear the ceremonial table and bring in our supper, called the *eumbok*, "eating the ancestor's blessings." We sit cross-legged on the floor, eating *boolgogi, paejeon, tteok,* and *bap* from communal bowls.

Dr. Nho kneels on the floor, props a *haegeum* between his knees, and plays a mournful tune which is done at all burials. Then he fills juice glasses with *soju*, sweet potato vodka, and we toast one another.

He rides the elevator down to the street with us to hail a cab. "In the past," he says, "we would travel to the gravesites several times a year to conduct the rituals, and usually we honored three or four generations. Now because of busy schedules and the number of Korean women working, most Koreans hold the ceremony in their homes."

He is silent for a moment. "Confucius said that, of all things brought about by ritual, harmony is the most valuable," he says. "Today, some order the ceremonial meal from online catering services and have the food delivered to their ancestors' graves. I worry that our children will not understand the importance of ceremony."

As he speaks of altering the ritual, I hear the sound of women laughing and chatting in the kitchen as they prepare potatoes and ham, coleslaw, and cakes for my mother's funeral. I smell egg coffee brewing in a pot. I remember how many times I have begged off from serving funeral lunches because of committee meetings and stacks of ungraded papers, how seldom I have tended to the graves in the cemetery back at Reliance, or have hired a floral shop to deliver flowers to my parents' graves on Memorial Day.

As I rode the train from Daejeon to Seoul, I always admired the graveyards nestled in the hollows of the hills, the tombs like little haystacks rising from grass. I imagined families standing at the gravesites, holding wrapping cloths filled with food, incense, and wine as children fulfilled their obligations to filial piety. But there were neglected gravesites overgrown with weeds and statuaries that listed toward the earth. There are lonely cemeteries in South Dakota as well, with crumbling tombstones and scraggly bushes.

On July 17, 2004, my mother died of congestive heart failure. That night as I drove north on Interstate 29, I felt a presence over my left shoulder. When I turned my head, I saw the clouds stretching across the horizon. The sunset flooded the clouds in a rich coral color. My mother loved color, and I knew she was in that radiant light. Behind her I could see a long line of my ancestors—my father, my grandparents, my aunts and uncles. Confucians value *hsiao,* paying homage to your ancestors, who are the source of your life. I was being called back to the graveyard in the grasslands, where I could perform a ceremony that honored my family.

When I was growing up, we lived in town during the school term and on the farm in the summer. During those months in town, Mother joined several koffee klatches, a whist club, the TOPS Club, and was the organist for Saint James Church. She didn't like being alone on the farm, and we knew she would not live there after my father died. So, we buried him in the nearest cemetery on the east bluff of the river in a graveyard where the grass is clipped and raked and where rectangular flat mounds of granite are ivories on a keyboard of grass and the wind is a funeral dirge.

In her later years, Mother's Lyman County roots grew stronger as her own life grew more fragile. She drove to Reliance for Sunday mass and coffee afterwards with family and old neighbors. She took flowers to the cemetery on Memorial Day, often decorating more than thirty graves. As her health deteriorated, we pondered her funeral arrangements and agreed we wanted to take her back to Reliance. But we were afraid to ask what she wanted because Mother believed that the death of an elderly person equaled abandonment by the doctors and the family.

"Why do you suppose she died, anyway?" she asked, puzzled at the death of a ninety-year-old relative. "I think everybody gave up on her."

We weren't brave enough to discuss funeral arrangements with her.

One day over a roast beef dinner at the Cracker Barrel, I asked what she thought about having her funeral at Saint Mary's and being buried in the Reliance Cemetery.

"Well," she said with the deadpan look she'd perfected over the years, "I'll have kicked the bucket, so I guess I don't care."

And when I asked if we could move our father to lie beside her, she said, "He'll be dead, too, so you may as well bring him along."

That was the sum total of my mother's contribution to her funeral plans.

We buried my mother in the Reliance Cemetery, where the tombstones scatter helter-skelter and the buffalo grass needs no tending. The next year, we moved our father from the cemetery on the river bluffs to lie beside her. On the anniversary of Mother's death, my family rented a hunting lodge overlooking the Missouri River. Thirty children, grandchildren, and great-grandchildren gathered for the weekend to lay our parents' tombstone.

The kitchen staff prepared a South Dakota *eumbok*, a buffet supper of our ancestors' blessings—beef, chicken, corn, green beans, mashed potatoes and gravy, and a cake to celebrate a new grandchild's July birthday.

We had a talent show. My brother Terry and his sons brought electric guitars, a bass, and a sound system powerful enough to blast the Grateful Dead and Van Morrison across the river bluffs. Brother Jim sang "Green Grass of Home" and "The Auctioneer's Song." Maura and my nieces put on skits. A four-year-old nephew named Sam captured the trophy by singing "Ring of Fire."

My brother Kevin recalled stories about our parents and our childhood escapades. We laughed until we cried and cried until we laughed again. Now it is our children who parent the next generation of the Woster and McManus clans. Perhaps the stories we told that night will be the common thread that connects them in the years to come.

When the show was over, we congregated around Mother's Impala, loaned to us for the weekend by the teenage girl who bought the car when my mother could no longer drive. The grandchildren remembered running to Grandma's car and springing open the trunk to pick out toys and board games from the stash she kept there. I recalled the car as the symbol of her independence and also the painful day she relinquished the keys. Just as the sun was beginning to drop over the river bluffs, we passed cameras to our cousin Red who stood on a balcony taking pictures of us. The flashbulbs were fireflies darting through the darkening sky. It was an evening worthy of being called an Irish wake.

The next morning, we drove over the river to the cemetery. With the help of a young cousin's front loader and robust grandsons, we lifted the black granite stone from my brother-in-law's truck bed to the loose dirt covering the graves. The stonecutter had etched a sheaf of wheat above my father's name and a Celtic cross above my mother's. A tiny ladybug cut in the stone crawled up the right side, a symbol of "The Ladybugs," the name the granddaughters gave the club they formed during summer visits with their grandma.

We wandered around reading names on the tombstones and telling stories about the person buried there. As I studied the names and listened to the tales of their lives, I considered how fifty years ago, I had been eager to leave this place and these people, believing anyplace else was better. Now I had been guided back to the landscape where my roots spread their tendrils deep and wide beneath the Lyman County soil.

We gathered in a circle around our parents' graves. Jim, the oldest son, stepped forward and said, "This feels right. It was good to bring our parents' home."

I read a Wendell Berry poem I had chosen to honor my father's eloquence: *He taught me sentences/ Outspoken fact for fact/ in swift coherences/ Discriminate and exact.*

And for my mother, a John Updike poem to capture her Pippi Longstocking spirit: *And another regrettable thing about death/ is the ceasing of your own brand of magic/ which took a whole life to develop and market.*

Terry led us in singing the Irish blessing: "May the road rise to meet you, may the wind be always at your back, may the sun shine warm upon your face." He continued in a shaky voice when the rest of us could not.

Just as he finished singing, a gust of wind blew across the graveyard and kicked up small whirlwinds of dust and the smell of withered grass. Tucked into the soil of a nearby tombstone, a bluebird whirligig spun its wings while overhead, a red-tailed hawk rose and fell in the updraft. From somewhere, a red-winged blackbird warbled.

The night before, as I danced around the room to "Good Morning, Little School Girl," I looked out the window to see a doe standing by the fence just a few yards away, sniffing the air and lifting her ears as if puzzled by the hard-driving beat of the bass. As I stood in this cemetery, I could feel the presence of the birds, the doe, the wind, and my family's spirits swirling around me, as if all had come to give witness to our parents' lives.

"In Laguna, when someone dies, you don't get over it by forgetting, you get over it by remembering," said Navaho writer Leslie Marmon Silko. Having witnessed a Korean ancestor veneration ceremony, I realized how easily the border between the living and spirit worlds collapses in the simple act of sharing meals, of picnics in cemeteries. Such moments reassure the dead that they are living members of their family and offer continuity among the generations present and to come.

We stood in silence, weeping, our arms around one another. Then, just as we were leaving, the sun broke out from behind a cloud and passed over the tombstone. In the bright light, the black granite was the color of spring clover.

Chapter Sixteen

I am standing in a small museum in Gyeongju, the capital of the Three Kingdoms era. The air in the chamber is so damp it tastes of fresh rain. Beneath the perfume of hyacinth is the smell of earth and stone; beneath the silence, the murmuring of prayers. A window opens to a statue of Kwan Seum Bosal, the Buddhist Madonna. She sits on a tufted cushion, one knee drawn to her chest. Her garment drapes from her shoulders to her lap to her bare feet, and a lotus blossom on a chain wraps around the folds of her neck. There is serenity in her Mona Lisa smile and a hint of recognition in eyes peering at me beneath her hooded lids.

The tour guide says quietly, "She is a *bodhisattva,* or realized being, who delays Nirvana until all world suffering is eradicated. She waits for those who are troubled to stand in the presence of her mercy and wisdom so we might leave with peace."

Kwan Seum extends her hand toward me as if to reach through the glass and touch my face. Candles bathe her limestone figure in honey-colored hues, and I imagine her hand would be warm against my cheek as I once imagined the Blessed Mother's hand warm against my scalp.

A *mala* dangles from the fingers of her other hand, provoking images of black, emerald green, gold, and silver rosaries falling in ovals from crucifixes on our walls. We tucked them in the corners of our nightstands and kitchen drawers, the glove compartments of our cars and trucks. One year I had a glow-in-the-dark rosary I hung from my mirror. It cast a garish light over my childhood bed until the light died and the room was dark again, a failure of the rosary's mystery that unsettled me.

My family prayed the rosary every day. In the living room, where I leaned against a footstool, my knees pressed against the linoleum; in the car, my back crunched between the glove compartment and my mother's knees, my head resting on her lap; at the communion railing beneath an alcove that housed a statue of the Virgin Mary, stars hovering above her. A white scarf covered her dark hair. A virgin-blue robe draped over the swell of her breasts and abdomen and kissed her bare feet.

Below her was a brass vase etched with wheat sheaves. In spring, the Altar Society ladies filled the vase with lilacs and peonies, in winter with evergreen branches and red carnations. A brass stand held rows of votive candles. My father gave us dimes to buy matches and light the candlewicks. We dropped the coins through a slot in a metal change box. Their clanging echoed across the chapel. In the flickering candlelight and the faint smell of melting wax, we fingered the beads as we prayed, "Hail Mary, full of grace. . . blessed is the fruit of thy womb."

It was 1975, and I was shivering in a paper gown as I fingered an invisible rosary with my thumb and index finger. I whispered, "Hail Mary, full of grace, Hail Mary full of grace."

Earlier, a nurse had wrapped a blood pressure cuff around my arm and pumped a rubber bulb. The dial bounced upward. I heard a sharp intake of breath. She pumped again, and then again. The cuff choked my arm so tightly my hand numbed. "I'll be right back," she said, and hustled out of the room. An examination I thought would be routine was blurred with frightening sensations—a tourniquet and a needle digging into my flesh, cold metal against my back, a camera's clicking, and the creeping awareness that something was very wrong.

The gynecologist came into the room. His hand moved slowly as if straining underwater toward black-and-white images on milky glass. I heard the whispers of crisp paper beneath my quivering legs, but I couldn't hear his words. He pointed to a dark blotch among white shadows, a kidney shriveled to the size of a walnut that would later be removed, leaving a twelve-inch gash across my back. The doctor's lips shaped words. "The damage done to your right kidney— probably the result of rheumatic fever—has left you with morbid hypertension. Your blood pressure reading today is 220/120."

I was pulled into an eddy of terror, but he clasped my hands and brought me to the surface with his quiet voice. "With your history of pre-eclampsia, should you become pregnant again, you will be at high risk for catastrophic problems."

I was twenty-eight when I was pregnant with Maura, a geriatric pregnancy in those days. In my eighth month, my blood pressure soared, and I began a weekly routine of blood pressure checks and urine analyses to detect protein that might indicate eclampsia. When he couldn't control the hypertension, the doctor induced labor. For twelve hours, I was strapped to the bed. An IV line dripped saline and anti-seizure medication in one arm. A blood pressure monitor was wrapped around my other arm. The machine inhaled and exhaled as if it too were in labor. Ken rubbed my back with lotion until his hands were stiff and chapped. The hands on the clock didn't move.

On January 29, 1973, Maura was born posterior, or face up, as if she couldn't wait to see what life held for her. Later that night, she lay beside me, her head nestled in the crook of my arm, her breath soft and rapid. I traced the curve of her lips with my finger, ran my thumb over her eyelashes and her tiny seashell ears. I was exhausted, happy, and fearful that my health scare wasn't over. The nurse came into the room and took my blood pressure. It was normal. The diagnosis was pregnancy-induced hypertension.

A year passed. Then one day, as I carried a basket of laundry up the stairs, I became so dizzy and short of breath that I had to sit on the step until the spell passed. A week later, the doctor looked me in the eyes and, choosing his words carefully, said, "We need to remove the damaged kidney. In the meantime, you must be certain you don't get pregnant again. But you shouldn't have the surgery. You've already been through enough. I think your husband needs to take care of this."

I drove home from the clinic as dusk was falling, the doctor's words cycling through my brain. "You might survive pregnancy or labor, but you may have a heart attack, seizures, or strokes that could cause permanent brain damage to either you or the baby, maybe both."

I started to cry, and my hands shook so that I couldn't grasp the steering wheel. I pulled over, leaned my head against the wheel, and sobbed. Cars swerved around me, horns blaring. I choked on diesel fumes from a truck rumbling by. Finally, I calmed myself and drove home. I walked into the house and into Ken's arms saying, "It's too dangerous for me to have another baby." He held me while I cried and then said, "I'll see the doctor and schedule my vasectomy."

In Tumuli Park, we stroll past grassy burial mounds that swell from the earth in an open plain not far from

Gyeongju. The tombs hold the bones and possessions of kings from the Silla Era. Cheonmachong, "the Heavenly Horse Tomb," the largest tomb in Tumuli Park, houses thousands of artifacts—gilded girdles, gold rings, gold plates, sabers, and a lacquered wooden coffin. But the centerpiece is a five-colored ceremonial saddle that dates back to the fifth or sixth century. The tumulus is a monument to an unknown king and the horse that was sacrificed and buried with him. An aura of maleness permeates the dusky cave. In the close, moist air, I feel as if I am suffocating. I reach for Ken's hand. "Let's get out of here."

Our tour guide leads us to an outdoor pavilion with metal railings around a massive bell covered with relief patterns of lotus flowers, grasses, and two *Apsarases*, heavenly maidens. It hangs from a dragon-shaped hook.

"This bell is called Seondeok Daewang Sinjong, The Divine Bell of the Great King Seondeok," she says. "On still days, its ringing can be heard for nearly forty miles."

According to legend the bell was cast three times. The first time it didn't ring; the second time, it cracked. The head priest at the temple had a dream that the fire dragon demanded the metal must be melted once again and the body of a small girl thrown into the molten metal before being recast. A village girl was chosen.

"It is also called the Emille Bell because of the mournful sound it makes when it is rung," she says. "Some say it is the child crying '*emille*' which means 'mother.'" She is quiet for a moment. "Of course, that is just a story, but a sad one."

In the green fragrance of pines, I imagine the smell of melting metal. In the laughter of children coming from a playground, I hear a child calling for her mother. I see a king smiling as the recast bell keeps its perfect shape. I reach for Ken's hand again, wrap my fingers around his.

In the weeks following Ken's vasectomy, I felt surrounded by wombs—pregnant women sitting with their legs splayed in the clinic waiting room, plastic wombs in the doctor's office, wombs on mannequins wearing maternity clothes in shop windows. I dreamt of wombs—glowing, moist, fertile wombs. We did not speak of vaginas, uteruses, or breasts in my childhood home, but we sanctified a woman's womb with our prayers. I knew of no prayers for fruitless wombs.

I was overwhelmed with the realization that I was a thirty-year-old woman whose health was so precarious I couldn't risk being pregnant. I endured bouts of depression, curled in a chair afraid to leave the house for fear I would have a heart attack or stroke. Panic attacks jerked me out of sleep, gasping for breath, my heart racing, and the dark closing in on me. What would happen to Maura if she woke one day to find her mother missing? What other woman could love her as I did? I felt for the rosary tucked beneath my pillow, but the beads slipped through my fingers.

Ken reached to pull me close, but I drew away. I was angry at him for seeming to move past the grief. At the same time, I didn't want to burden him with my sadness; at least that's what I told myself. In truth, I didn't give Ken a chance to help, although I'm not sure why. He was not a cradle Catholic, so he had never heard sermons warning against the evil of birth control. Perhaps I didn't trust his logical Protestant perspective to understand my unexpected and irrational belief that suffering was my penance for my sin.

Needing affirmation that we made the right choice, I called a Catholic woman I had known for several years. "Hi, Helen," I said. "I really need to talk. I just found out I have morbid hypertension and can't get pregnant again, so Ken had a vasectomy."

There was a long silence on the line. In the living room, Maura sang "I Love Trash" with Oscar the Grouch. I could see her curled up on the carpet in front of the television, her favorite quilt tucked under her head.

"What did you say?"

I repeated my words.

Another silence. Her breathing was soft on the line between us. Why wasn't she saying something? "He actually had a vasectomy?"

"The doctor said. . . I might. . ." I stammered. "Maybe a seizure or stroke or death."

I tried to make sense of her response, but I couldn't.

"Well, I'm shocked. I can't believe you would agree to his having a vasectomy."

I hung up the phone, slid down the wall, and curled in on myself, becoming smaller and smaller and as brittle as milkweed in August. The next week the woman sent a note that read, "I don't know what you wanted me to say. I was just so stunned at your news."

I wanted this woman to be my Kwan Seum, born in the tears that Buddha shed when he witnessed the pain of the world. I wanted her to say, "I'm sorry, this must be so difficult for you." To extend her hand toward me in mercy and reassure me that I was more than a tragic but necessary casualty in the imperative of procreation. I wanted her to tell me that I had value beyond my womb.

I telephoned my mother. When I heard her voice sliding over the thin but resilient cord that connects mother to daughter no matter how far the distance, I began to sob.

"What's wrong?" I could see her holding the phone tight against her ear, her mind racing with possibilities. Had someone died? Was her granddaughter safe?

I told her about the doctor's diagnosis.

"Well, if you get pregnant, you will have an abortion," my Irish Catholic mother said. "You have a little girl. It would be irresponsible to risk leaving her."

Those were the words she spoke, but the words I heard were, "You are the child of my womb. Your life matters."

A few weeks later, I walked through a line of people crowding the sidewalk in front of my gynecologist's clinic. They carried placards with magnified images of fetuses. Some fingered rosaries, their lips moving. Others sang softly. Words on the signs blurred as I passed by them—Choose life, Holocaust, Butcher. The last was meant for the gynecologist I was scheduled to see.

I didn't know until then that my doctor was the only one to perform abortions in South Dakota. I had deep reservations about abortion and never wanted to be in a position where I had to make such a choice. Yet, I understood the fears that might drive a woman to choose to have one, why a doctor might perform one. I suspect my doctor held many women's hands, the way he once held mine, as they cried over traumatic pregnancies. He was an advocate for women. When I told him Ken had a vasectomy, he grinned and pumped his fist. "Yes, that's the kind of man I like. A man generous enough to make that choice."

I continued to see the doctor even after the protests started, but the marches grew more frequent and the lines longer. I began to dread the walk past the signs, the soft murmuring of the rosary, the beads dangling from fingertips. Eventually I didn't have the courage to face the crowds, or perhaps I was too unsettled by the thought of abortions performed in that clinic. Despite his kindness to me, I changed doctors.

The guide leads us into a dimly-lit gallery where stone statues of Buddha perch on pedestals. Some wear top knots on their large heads and others have snail-shell curls. A few figures press their hands together in meditation while others rest their hands palms up on their laps. All have jagged holes in their faces where their noses should be. "Did erosion create these holes?" someone asks the guide.

She shakes her head. "No. Women once believed that eating Buddha's nose assured they would bear sons, so they hacked the noses off statues, ground the pieces into a powder, and mixed it with their food." She seems both sad and embarrassed at revealing this information.

She walks toward the next gallery, stops, turns around, and says, "I will tell you that abortion is illegal in Korea, but many are performed. We just don't talk about it."

It is also illegal to tell expectant parents the gender of their child, but she believes many doctors do reveal that information and that some abortions are performed to guarantee the birth of a boy. "Having a son is very important in this country, for it is sons, not daughters, who care for parents in their old age."

She sighs and shrugs her shoulders. "I, of course, am the mother of three daughters." Her bronze-colored eyes darken. Did she feel responsible for the genetics of gender the way I had once felt guilty for being the mother of an only child, proof of my defective womb? In the 1950s, when I was a young girl, the Church encouraged women to be open to accepting children from God—many children. I heard whispers about mothers who had only one child. "She's just selfish."

In the last years of Mother's life, she lived in Sioux Falls, only an hour away from Brookings. We often had lunch at a small café overlooking Phillips Avenue. One day, out of the blue, she said, "I thought the babies would never quit coming." She tugged at her grilled cheese sandwich with gnarled fingers, tore off a bit of bread, and chewed the piece slowly.

"When your father went to bed, I would tell him that I had stay up to iron the clothes or mix the dough for the refrigerator buns. He was so frustrated with me."

I picked up a ceramic creamer, poured half and half into my coffee, and studied the stream swirling into the dark liquid, afraid that if Mother looked into my eyes she would remember where she was and what she was revealing. She looked out the window at the cars inching down the narrow street. "I always thought I wanted ten children, maybe more. But eventually I realized that I couldn't keep having babies."

We were silent for a moment, untangling our memories into the separate yet common threads woven into lives of mothers and daughters. The sun shining through the restaurant's window deepened the hollows in the corners of her eyes and made shadows on her neck. Yet in its light, her face, despite age and ill health, was smooth as a young girl's.

Mother said, "I told your father that the day will come when Catholic couples will ignore Church rule and practice birth control."

Her prediction was right. During our prenuptial preparation, the campus priest had said, "If having a baby means Ken has to drop out of college to support a family, then you need to think about using contraceptives until you can afford a child."

When I told her that she looked surprised, but she nodded her head. "That's good. Well, I wouldn't give up one of my children. But it makes me furious to think that I had to worry all those years about getting pregnant."

Like a farmer planting the fields, Mother often tossed seeds of stories into our conversation. That day I learned that my mother, who worried that the babies would never quit coming, was forbidden by the Church to practice birth control, and that her maneuvers to avoid sex may have strained her marriage.

"What did Dad say about the Church's ban on birth control?"

She jerked her head toward me, her hazel eyes darkening. "Why can't you leave well enough alone?"

I'm not sure why she cut me off. As a Catholic man of his generation, I'm certain my father accepted the ban on contraception the way he accepted other rules imposed by the Church. As the man of the house, he had the final decision. Perhaps she didn't want to admit there was tension between them. She may have wanted to shelter my father's memory from his feminist daughter's ire. It's also possible she was protecting the church the way she protected her family. She might privately criticize her children, but she would never tolerate others doing so.

Mother sighed, shook her head, and looked down at the floor, the familiar signal that our talk was over.

A few weeks later, my priest, fresh out of the seminary, focused his sermons on feminists who "made enemies of children" by advocating for reproductive rights. One day he declared from the height of the lectern, "Women who

use contraceptives are more likely to be unfaithful t
husbands because their marriage is based on a lie."

He looked around the room at each couple before
adding, "Husbands do not respect wives who practice the
sinful use of contraception." What did he know of my
marriage? How dare he judge? Despite my anger, I felt the
old shame and guilt of using contraception wash over me.
That night, I dreamed I was walking into the foyer of the
church, where women tiny as marionettes spun like
pinwheels, their eyes wide, their mouths pursed in perfect
circles, as if they were screaming "oh" but no sound came
from them. They whirled past men in black robes huddled
in a circle. When I woke up, the sheets were wound around
me as tightly as a shroud. I heard someone whisper, "I can't
do this anymore." The voice was mine.

Not long after our tour of Tumuli Park, I hunch over a
computer in our Korean apartment and read about a bill
the South Dakota Legislature is considering that would ban
all abortions except in cases where the mother might die.
Kwan Seum, in a blood-red gown tinged in gold and with a
lotus flower blossoming on her head, hovers from a shelf
above me. She holds a scroll in one hand. Her other hand
shapes the *mudra* for calling the earth to witness.

South Dakota politicians argue over an exception that
allowed abortions if pregnancy posed serious health risks for
the mother. One man declares a woman might use a possible
risk to her health as a convenient loophole so she could have
an abortion. A clergyman says that a doctor's diagnosis is never
one hundred percent certain. "Perhaps the mother would not
suffer serious harm," he said. I flinch when I read the words
of a bishop: "A woman's life must never be preferred over the
life of the child," by which he means the fetus.

I remember how the tourists gasped when the tour
guide in Gyeongju said, "Visit any elementary classroom
and you will find a disproportionate number of boys to
girls." We can be horrified at female feticide, but we
shouldn't be shocked. Screening for sons is the legacy of
societies where women once choked on stone so they might
bear sons and legends are told of tossing young girls into
hot metal to fulfill a man's wishes. The subtext of laws that
endanger a woman's health and the words of clergy that
defend such laws is that women are indeed disposable.

My computer keyboard rattles as I type a letter to a
political reporter to ask if my medical history would qualify

for an abortion under this law. I punch the send button. Later that day, I receive the reporter's emailed response. "As the bill reads right now, you could not legally end the pregnancy. But you could probably go to court and win your case to have an abortion."

I see a courtroom where lawyers circle tables, depositions in hand, words flying around me—morbid hypertension, failed kidneys, abortion of convenience, murder. On a raised platform, a man in a black robe and stiff, white collar listens to the words that will determine if my life has meaning beyond the delivery room. Ultimately the South Dakota legislature will pass a bill with no exception for the mother's health, but the law will be overturned a few months later in a special election.

For over thirty years, I was silent about my health problems and subsequent battle with depression and anxiety. I was sad, of course, but I was also ashamed, as if I'd failed somehow. Nor could I risk another rejection like the one I felt the day I called a friend to say I couldn't have more children. But I won't be silent anymore. On my return to South Dakota, armed with the words of a Korean proverb, *When a woman is bent on unraveling the knot in her heart, she can cover the sky in July with snow,* I will attend strategy meetings to defeat the abortion bill. I will stand up and say "This is about women being valued beyond their wombs." My hands will shake and the words will come in spurts, but I will tell my story, and the women who listen will not judge me.

I leave my desk, walk across the room, and look out the open window at the hills that circle the CNU campus. In the sunlight, the patches of snow between pine trees sparkle. I remember the tour guide's words, "Kwan Seum is a shapeshifter who can become whatever form brings peace to the supplicant—a thin-mustached man in red trousers, a goddess with a thousand arms extended in mercy, an androgynous figure with eyes in the palms of its hands to see the suffering of the world."

I close my eyes and see Kwan Seum sitting placidly on her lotus blossom, her hand reaching for me. "Now," the guide says, "place your hands over your eyes, lean against the window, and position your hands so that all you can see is her figure. See how her posture suggests stillness, how even her hands shape the *mudra* that says be still, be at peace."

I lace my fingers and press them against the glass. I block out the pillow and the stone wall. For a moment I focus on the beads wrapped around her hand, recalling the smell of candles and carnations in a small chapel. I see a woman's blue robe falling in soft folds over her body. I hear the clanging of coins echoing through silence.

"Slowly close your fingers until everything disappears and only her eyes remain."

I squeeze my fingers tighter until I can see only Kwan Seum's eyes gazing back at me. I wait, expecting nothing and yet everything.

"Now do you understand?" the woman whispers. "Kwan Seum is telling you that when you offer empathy to others, you release yourself from self-judgment and guilt. You learn to love yourself. And then *tathagatagarbhaa*, the seed of compassion, can take root and flower in you."

Tears pool in the corners of my eyes, perhaps from focusing so intently on her face, her eyes, so that I might achieve *ivipasyan*, that moment when the observer becomes the observed. A candle sputters and its blue flames flash over the statue. Kwan Seum's eyes turn blue in the light, as if my eyes are looking back at me with the fullness of mercy.

I blink, and my eyes are clear.

Chapter Seventeen

A Buddhist monk draped in a taupe-colored robe and brown sandals enters Birojeon, the Hall of Enlightenment, bringing with him a whiff of sun-kissed linen. Trousers balloon above his thin ankles, and the sleeves of his tunic flutter as he bends over to undo the sandal straps. His bald head and the wire-rimmed glasses that cover his eyes and eyebrows flatten his face somehow as if he has no distinguishing features. Then I see the tiny nose, delicate hands, and the swell of breasts beneath the robe. "Ken," I whisper. "That's a *bhiksuni.*"

I had just read about Buddhist nuns, how they prepare to become nuns by studying the *sutras*, meditating, and gardening in mountaintop temples. On the day of their ordination they bathe from two bowls—one for upper body, one for the lower—shave their heads, and don robes. They go to the temple, where they kneel and chant for hours.

In a slow, fluid motion, she coils inward as if walking an internal labyrinth and kneels before Buddha, whose hands shape the *mudra* of enlightenment. She hunches, presses her hands against the floor, and rests her forehead on them. I, too, have knelt on cold stone, my back bent with the weight of guilt against my spine. But her posture suggests not remorse, rather a curling in on herself, as if to explore what lies within. I watch her for several minutes.

In the light of candles, the landscape of delicate bones beneath the pale skin of the *bhiksuni's* scalp is translucent and makes her somehow both exposed and yet closeted, strong yet vulnerable, male yet female. Is there some kind of power in androgyny, something liberating in being unencumbered by a woman's sexuality? But before I can follow that train of thought, I am derailed by memories of a young girl who was defined by the names others bestowed on her.

Exposed roots of trees clutch dirt banks along a rocky trail hugging the side of Mt. Toham. I hike this path to

Seokguram Grotto, a cave carved into the mountainside that houses one of South Korea's national treasures—a massive limestone statue of Buddha. The grotto is my first stop before entering Birojeon Hall in Bulguksa Temple below, a place where I hope to cleanse my spirit, perhaps even still what some Buddhists call "a monkey mind," that jungle of jittery thoughts which has kept me unfocused and nervous for much of my life.

It is the Festival of Lights, Buddha's birthday, and people walk the path carrying candles in lotus blossom holders. I follow behind several Buddhist monks who walk in meditation so slowly that only their pewter-hued *kesas* swirling around their ankles seem to be in motion. The air is crisp, the sky brilliant with possibilities. The sea below shimmers, reflecting the sun's light like stars in morning skies, stars as bright as the one that awakened Siddhartha Guatama more than two millennia ago.

Born a wealthy prince from Kapilavastu in Northern India, Buddha sat for seven days and nights under the heart-shaped leaves of a fig tree, wrestling with a *koan* as twisted as the gnarled trunk. What is the cause of *dukkha*? On the morning of the eighth day of the last month of the lunar year, he found the answer in the clarity of a star. "The root of all suffering is desire," he proclaimed. He rejected his family name and wealth, left his wife and child, and spent the rest of his life meditating and practicing non-attachment. He became known as Buddha, the Awakened One.

There are many ways to choose a name for a child. Some read books of names or hire naming consultants. Catholics often choose a saint's name. I found Maura's name in the back of a *Webster's New Dictionary*. For Buddhists, the custom of giving a *dharma* name is something like the Native American tradition. The name may reflect phenomena witnessed at the child's birth. Or the name may be earned through ritual or achievement, or in my case, by simply being born.

I was born in St. Joseph Catholic Hospital on the eighth day of the last month in 1945. I am told that my mother, woozy from ether and the exhaustion of a long labor, thought she was dreaming when she was stirred from her sleep by the sound of rubber soles gliding over tile floors and the clicking of rosary beads against leather belts. When she awakened to a curtain of black draped over her bed and a circle of celestial faces beaming down on her, I imagine her thinking, "Henry, I told you that one day, mark my words, if I keep having babies it will kill me." I even imagine her feeling vindicated that her prediction had at last come true.

But the nuns had come to admire the girl-child born on the Feast of the Immaculate Conception, a Catholic holy day that celebrates Mary's freedom from original sin, the stain on our souls washed away by the waters of baptism.

"And so, Mrs. Woster," one sister might have asked, "what is the child's middle name to be?"

"Ruth. Her middle name will be Ruth," my mother said, her etherized voice sliding over the sloping edges of vowels.

"Oh, Mary Ruth," the nun cooed, making the sign of the cross on my forehead as I slept in my mother's arms. "What a lovely name."

"No, Alice Ruth."

A few years later, I sat on the floor with crayons and coloring book while my mother bent over the piano, her fingers suspended above the keys for just a second between arpeggios as she sang, "In her sweet little Alice Blue gown." She stopped, turned to me, and said, "I love that song. You know, I wanted to name you Alice."

I was stunned. I was supposed to have a different name? "Mom, why did you change your mind?"

"Oh, I don't know."

She brushed her fingers lightly over the keys, playing a melody only she heard. "The nuns said that Mary was more appropriate, I guess." Her smile seemed pinched, and a hint of shadow fell over her eyes.

"Oh, no, no, no, Mrs. Woster," the nun might have said, shaking her head, jowls and veil jiggling. "This child's birth honors the Blessed Virgin. Her name will be Mary, the Beloved Lady. The middle name may be your choice."

"But weren't you mad at the nuns?"

She shrugged her shoulders. "It was no big deal." Only a Catholic woman of my mother's generation would so easily relinquish the right to name her daughter and then deny resenting the sisters for making her do so. She turned back to the piano and sang a particularly jazzy version of "Five Foot Two, Eyes of Blue."

Perhaps I only imagine that moment because Mother's most intimate conversations came when her hands were busy—cooking, doing dishes, playing the piano. I do remember how the revelation unsettled me. Would I be a different girl if I were Alice? But I never asked her again about changing my name. My mother's evasions were the *koans* I wrestled with for much of my life.

So my mother took the pen the nun offered and in her compact cursive wrote the name Mary Alice on my birth certificate.

That was my first *dharma* name.

Only a Catholic girl of my age would appreciate the cachet my birthday gave me. It was a day that obliged all Catholics to attend mass, and so it began at dawn as I knelt in the pew and thought of people around the world—Italy, Africa, Brazil, and even perhaps communist Russia— gathering to pray and to sing, "Immaculate Mary, Your Praises we sing. Ave, Ave, Ave Maria."

Birthday gifts were crystal rosaries, leather mass books, holy cards, and once, a sterling silver medal engraved with the image of Mary, her robe embossed in blue glaze. She stood on a globe with turquoise seas and green continents, her bare feet crushing the head of a snake. Rays of light flashed from her outstretched hands. Although the chain left red bumps on my neck and collar bone, I wore the medal for years.

Even the nuns paused and smiled when they read my name in Catechism class. "Mary. What a lucky girl. You are Mary, the Beloved Child."

That was my second *dharma* name.

A diamond flashed on his heavy-knuckled finger as Father John jabbed the air. "You girls are occasions of sin." This was my third *dharma* name.

I sat on a folding chair along with other teenage girls, my head lowered and my hair veiling my face. I felt hot with shame. "If a boy has sexual feelings because of you girls or if he is aroused by the way you dress or sit, even if you do not have sex, you have caused him to sin. And that is grave offense against God."

A white collar pressed in the folds of his drooping jowls. His cheeks were flushed and his bushy eyebrows furrowed as he looked from one girl to the next. "You were born with the stain of original sin on your soul. But there were no black marks on the Blessed Virgin's soul. She was pure from the moment she was conceived."

After Catechism class, I crept into the dim sanctuary, dipped my fingers in a puddle of holy water, and blessed myself. I knelt at Mary's feet, the marble step cold against my knees, and hunched over the communion railing. The roof creaked, and votive candles flickered in the wind, casting fire over her sandstone image. White carnations drooped in a brass vase near the candles. There was a metallic and dusty smell. I heard Father's words echoing through the silence. "All her life Mary remained the Virgin Unsullied."

I couldn't look at the statue as I prayed, "Dear Mary, please don't let me be an occasion of sin tonight."

I left the church, climbed into a boy's Chevy, and hugged the passenger door as we drove to a bluff overlooking the river. He parked, turned the volume on the radio up, and pleaded with me until I slid over the vinyl seat and into the curve of his arms. Paul Anka crooned "Put Your Head on My Shoulder" as we moved toward something so sweet and seductive I yearned to see it to its conclusion. But when he fumbled with my buttons, I saw Father John in shadows as I confessed to the ways I was touched or kissed. I pulled away.

"God, you're such a cock tease," the boy muttered, bestowing on me my fourth *dharma* name. He cranked the engine and pushed hard on the gas pedal, spraying pebbles that pinged against the hubcaps as we drove away.

Saturday afternoons, I knelt in the confessional clenching a rosary. Sweat dampened my blouse under my arms and the back of my neck. My *mudra* was knees against a narrow board, elbows pressed against a shelf, and a face buried in hands. I strained to hear Father's voice beneath the murmuring coming from within the booth. Did he sound patient? Angry? There was the clunking of wood slamming against wood as Father opened the latticed window between us.

"Bless me, Father, for I have sinned. I French-kissed my boyfriend and let him touch my breasts four nights this week." Specifics seemed important to Father John.

My mantra was, "Please Father, don't look at me. Don't look at me."

He leaned his elbow on the arm of a high-backed chair, his fleshy cheek in the palm of one hand, his shoulders slumped, a *mudra* of despair at such a sinful girl. He sighed heavily. "For your penance say the rosary three times and do not tempt boys again." That was his mantra on Saturday afternoons.

Did Father John ever kneel in the dark, confronting his own potential to be an occasion of sin? Or did he twist his guilt into the shape of the girls in his class? Attachment,

Buddha taught, is the root of suffering. Why did I cling to the guilt and shame of being a woman instilled in me in that dark booth? Wear it like a sack cloth?

Why did I so easily accept that I was Mary, the Virgin Sullied, my fifth *dharma* name?

My freshman year at the university, I went to confession at the Newman Center. The priest gently opened the window, making no jarring sound of wood against wood. He was a slight man with thick, black-rimmed glasses, a Germanic nose, and hair swept back from his face. A greasy hint of Brylcreem hung in the air. I began to recite a list I long ago memorized—bodies tangled in a car, hands exploring forbidden places—but he interrupted me. "I'm really more interested in how you treated other people this week. Have you ignored someone in pain? Have you destroyed someone's soul with your gossip?"

I couldn't answer his questions. We were off script. What did gossip have to do with sin?

He turned toward me, willing me to look at him. His brown eyes were soft behind the gauzy curtain that separated us. "Look, confession is not about reading a grocery list of sins, and sins of desire are not the only sins we commit. Confession should be a chance to contemplate how we might demonstrate Christ's compassion in our dealings with others."

I nodded my head but still couldn't speak.

He made the Sign of the Cross saying, "For your penance, consider ways that you can be kind to others and to yourself, and reflect on the wisdom you have within you to do the right thing."

I felt the ground shift beneath me.

My long feet wobble over narrow stones shoved haphazardly into the hill that leads to the grotto. When I step into the dim entryway my stomach knots with the shame instilled in me by dark spaces. Then, as my eyes slowly adjust from the bright sun to this dusky room, I see a glowing statue of Buddha sitting on a pedestal in a key-hole-shaped chamber. His image is so incandescent I think it's a trick, a hologram perhaps. But it is the floodlights that illuminate the stone with a warm light. A garment drapes over one shoulder and across his lap. Pendulous ears touch his shoulders, reminders of the weight of his wealth in the gold earrings he once wore. In the middle of his forehead is a bump from which flows wisdom. His webbed fingers, fishing nets with which to capture his followers, shape the *mudra* of knowledge.

A *bhiksuni* enters the chamber and kneels at the base of Buddha's statue. Her robe pools around her ankles and the fabric blends into the dust-colored tile, exposing only the bottoms of her feet, pale and somehow vulnerable. I see another woman dressed in black lying on marble steps, her black oxfords twisted around one another.

I was twelve years old that day in August when I rode over a heat-buckled highway with my cousin and aunt and uncle to watch Peggy, a red-haired girl from our parish, profess her religious vows. I felt as if I were riding toward my destiny, for not only had the sisters at St. Joseph's named me, they petitioned the nuns at the Sisters of the Presentation of the Blessed Virgin Mary Convent to pray for my vocation. I was told that my name was written in a book near the altar, but I think that wasn't true.

My aunt gave us minced ham sandwiches and potato chips, and passed around a water jug of grape Kool-Aid. "We won't have time for lunch today, so we're eating early." Then she handed us rosaries with black beads. "Let's pray that one day you girls will also take the veil."

When I asked my mother why she wasn't coming to the convent with us, she pushed hard on the edges of a pie crust she was crimping and mumbled, "It's the harvest time, and I need to cook for your father." But I saw how her eyebrows pressed in brackets of fine hair above her nose. There was something in the way her shoulders pulled inward that was both penitent and rebellious, like the wings on the fallen angel in a picture hanging in the church basement.

Unlike many Catholic mothers of that time, she did not wish to raise a priest or a nun. On Vocation Sundays, she stood and prayed with the congregation, "Lead them to the vineyards where they will labor in God's holy service." But when I talked about the day I would join the convent, she said, "You don't have to become a nun just because somebody is praying you will. You vow to be dead to your family, you know. You even have to give up your name. That's ridiculous."

When I was a little girl, I often daydreamed about nuns kneeling over cots in their cells, fingering beads as they petitioned God to bring me to them. It was a romantic notion, a chance to be the bride of Christ and yet a virgin like Mary, although I didn't know what the word meant. As a child, I thought it was a title, like "Mrs." before a married woman's name. In junior high, I pieced together the contradiction of the virgin birth and the most horrifying insight, my first moment of *satori*: Mother had five children. I worked up the courage to ask her one day, "Mom, how can Mary be both a mother and a virgin."

"It was a miracle," she said, keeping her back to me as she folded tuna into noodles and mushroom soup. "Just don't worry about it."

Peggy wore a white gown cut in straight lines that hugged her curves, the scalloped neckline trimmed in lace. Her veil could not contain her fiery curls nor mask the lively blue eyes above a scattering of freckles. She was my dream of every bride who ever walked down the aisle, focused on her lover waiting for her. I willed her to look at me and know that one day I would join her. But she seemed oblivious to me; oblivious to the sun shining through the sepia-toned windows and bathing the chapel in amber; to the scent of ferns, lilies, and incense; and even to chants of nuns and to each lovely, haunting note suspended in the smoky air of the sanctuary.

The Mother Superior placed a piece of black wool folded like a flag into Peggy's hands. She left the chapel holding it in front of her as tenderly as a mother bringing her baby to the baptismal font. When she returned as Sister Mary Joseph, she was wrapped in black—gown, veil, and oxfords with long laces. Only her pale face, squished round as a pumpkin by her wimple, and her hands peeking from beneath woolen sleeves were exposed.

She seemed so boyish. Hips and breasts pressed into flat, angular lines, perhaps by the stays and buttons of undergarments. There was no hint of red curls. What lay beneath her veil? Would my head be shaved when I entered the convent? When I got home that night, I stood in front of the mirror, tucked my hair under a scarf, and pulled it tight. My eyes seemed even smaller and my acne more pronounced without hair. I could think of no greater sacrifice to offer God.

When I was in high school, a nun came to Catechism class to talk about vocations with the girls. I asked her why nuns shaved their heads.

"We don't shave our heads. We just cut our hair very short." I remembered the sensation of my boyfriend's fingers tangled in my hair as he leaned in to kiss me.

"Hair is a woman's greatest vanity," the nun continued. "Giving up our hair is symbolic of giving up all our worldly possessions and surrendering to something greater than ourselves."

All those nights in that parked car, I had resisted surrendering to my desires, to some mystery I could not understand. If I became a nun I would never know how those nights might have ended. Perhaps cutting my hair was not the greatest sacrifice God demanded of me.

When Sister Mary Joseph bowed before the altar, the sleeves of her habit ruffled like the feathers of a bird taking flight. But she didn't fly away; rather, she lay face down on the steps, her arms extended. She was an inverse image of the crucified Christ hanging above her, to whom she had offered her life. I felt the edges of the steps cut into my breasts and hip bones. Did she, too, feel stone against flesh or had her body been hardened by some inverse miracle inherent in her vow of celibacy? In losing her womanly flesh, was she now barren? A startling thought came to me. Would I exist if my mother had become a nun? What of the children I wouldn't bear?

In the 1960's, Sister Mary Joseph would join the exodus of women leaving the convent and move to a city where she met a man. My cousin would marry and raise five children, disappointing her mother, I suspect. If celibacy closed the door on their vocations, it may have opened doors for *bhiksuni*. Celibacy freed them from the Confucian tradition that required that women be subordinate to fathers, husbands, and then sons. *Bhiksuni* live in their own monasteries, separate from the rule of monks. Many are lavishly supported by their followers and so have money to travel on lecture tours, retreats, and pilgrimages to the birthplace of Buddhism and to fulfill their mission of teaching and serving the poor. As for me, I would walk down the aisle toward the blue-eyed man waiting for me at the altar.

I would renounce my sixth *dharma* name, Mary, the Bride of Christ.

I follow the trail back down the hill to Bulguksa Temple. In the courtyard, children chase one another beneath an upside-down garden of hollyhock-pink and sunflower-yellow lanterns strung on wires overhead. Vendors sell figurines of Buddha, wooden *malas*, ink rubbings of temples and lotus ponds, as well as *pajeon* and *sujeonggwa*, pancakes and ginger punch. I am jarred by the chaos, for I had counted on the silence of a sacred space to inspire meditation.

I find silence in Birojeon Hall, where the fragrance of wildflowers in celadon vases, the vibrant colors of lotus blossoms and dragons painted on the wooden beams, and the *bhiksuni* kneeling at the feet of Buddha might suggest that he is a deity. But Buddha never saw himself as a God. He never admonished his followers to think or to be like him. In the way that the priest at the Newman Center had counseled me to seek my own wisdom, Buddha encouraged people to ask questions and to reflect on the answers. Through quiet reflection, he taught, we might come to realize that within all of us is a being that is capable of meditating under the Bodhi Tree in search of enlightenment.

I glance around the room to see if others are watching. But they are absorbed in their own meditation, bending deeply at the waist or kneeling on the floor. I close my eyes and, in a clumsy attempt at *gassho*, fold my hands over my breasts and bend low in front of Buddha. I focus on emptying my thoughts and slowing my breathing. But my mind is jittery. The *bhiksuni* chants softly, words that sound something like *om santi, santi, santi*. Her bald head catches the light of candles. Buddhist nuns shave their heads not only to reject vanity and sexuality but also to shed ignorance. Have I, a Westerner and a cradle Catholic, come to this place to shed my ignorance? Or perhaps I have come to earn my own *dharma* name—Mary, the Seat of Wisdom.

I breathe deeply and take a hard swipe at the monkeys. I whisper a prayer, "May the calm of this place bring an end to worry and sadness. May all of us reach the shore of enlightenment together." But the monkeys keep jumping. For now.

I leave the hall and walk the path down the hill, over a stone arch bridge, past children in yellow tunics walking two by two, chattering like birds, their faces cheerful as sunflowers. The air is heavy with the smell of ripening tree buds and the salt of moist ocean breezes. Shoots of grass, celery green in the sun, pepper the hillsides. Above me, geese fly in a v-shaped formation, returning to their nesting sites in the north, the *mudra* of renewal. I walk beneath the branches of willow trees and past a lotus pond where white blossoms rest on heart-shaped pods. Their reflections fan out across the still water in starbursts of light.

CHAPTER EIGHTEEN

The "mother line". . . the successive generations
of women. . .who believe in you well before you
exist. . . and remember long after you are gone,
—Debra Marquardt, *The Horizontal World*

Buggy eyes emerge from the white caps and a snake-like figure bounces around a buoy the way seals at Sea World toy with rubber balls. A dolphin, I think, or perhaps a seal. I can't tell from this distance. The sun shining through mist casts a sheen over the water, and I remember rainbows of oil over puddles in our tool shed and my mother's words: "Don't ever drink that water! It's poison." It was both beautiful and disturbing to know that something dangerous floated above the surface of a substance that sustained me.

Jeanne and I are standing on a cliff overlooking the coastline of Jeju-Do, an island off the southern coast of Korea, where the East Sea intersects with the Sea of China. Jeanne reads from the guide book. "Jeju is called Samdado, the Island of Three Abundances: strong wind, strong rocks, strong women."

The barren, rocky coast stretches for miles. "You'd have to be rugged to live here," Jeanne says, her coat flapping in wind so wild and raw I feel it might lift me up and drop me in a tidal pool where I will be a jellyfish wriggling among sponges and sea anemones, flukes and mollusks.

Behind me, Seongsan Mountain, Sunrise Peak, thrusts through the basalt flats of Jeju Island. It is a volcanic crater that erupted more than one hundred thousand years ago. Ken and the guide who drove us around the island that day are climbing this mountain along with many pilgrims who have come to offer prayers to Seolmundae Halmang. She is the earth goddess who sits at the top of the peak, imposing order and harmony on the universe by weaving night and day, sea and sky, sound and light into a single cloth. The jagged edges of the crater and the slopes covered in golden rapeseed are the crown she wears.

Black tentacles come out of the sea and writhe above the surface. I squint and see that they are hands encased in rubber. One hand lifts swim goggles to a woman's brow, and a face leathered by sun and salt appears. Small breasts strain against a wet suit. "My God, Jeanne, look, that's a *haenyeo*."

I had already read about the sea women whose ancestors fished these waters for seafood and kelp using only a wet suit, goggles, and fins, but I didn't expect to see one. There is a shrill whistling sound, the *sumbisori* she makes by inhaling deeply and then exhaling with a force that expands the lungs like gills. The woman rises above the water's surface and then plunges into the sea. Her fins are exclamation points marking the place where she breaks through water.

A *haenyeo* can stay underwater for two minutes, a skill taught by her mothers and grandmothers and women before them. I watch circles radiate from the spot where the sea woman disappeared. I hold my breath, waiting for her black form to reemerge.

"What will we do if she doesn't come up? I can't call for help." I am beginning to panic.

Words were my profession, but my facility with language was useless in Korea. I couldn't make sense of the Hangul characters and could remember only a handful of useful phrases I memorized before we left South Dakota. "Help, someone is drowning," wasn't among those phrases.

Then the water breaks again, and a rubbery arm thrusts an octopus in the air, triumphant. The sea woman is safe. She drops the octopus in a net and clings to the *taewak*, a Styrofoam float I thought was a buoy. Then she slips back into the sea.

I imagine her punching down through the water, the weights tied to her waist both resisting and acquiescing to the water's pressure. She dives until she reaches the ocean's bottom, where the light dissolves into crystals of green. As she glides through the slag and seaweed, weaving through the light and shadows, does she hear her ancestors singing a *haenyeo Nojeooneun Sori*, a rowing song that tells of their labor? Does she pause to see the beauty in the burnished-gold kelp that clings to stone, in the lavender-speckled rocks, and in the sea urchins that cover the ocean floor like a bed of faded marigolds? Or is she thinking of how her work never ends and how in the morning, once again, drawn by the moon goddess DaeSoon to the fertile tides she will paddle her boat out to sea singing a *haenyeo* song before disappearing into the dark water?

*   *   *

My mother crept down the steep steps of the storm cellar carved into the dirt hill, alert and nervous. "I was always terrified to go down to the cellar alone," she once said. "I never knew what waited for me in that dark cave."

No doubt spiders and beetles scuttled over the dirt walls. Perhaps a garter snake slithered across the floor or a mouse scurried into a hole. Or her greatest fear, a rattlesnake coiled in the dark, his warning the sound of a wire brush whisking against the skin of a drum. When the candles were lit and the dangers dissipated, did she sit on a wooden bench with her back against the cool dirt and admire how the flickering candles transformed the rows of canning jars into jewels in glass cases—ruby-red beets, jade-green beans, pearls of onions, and layers of beef dark as onyx? Did my mother, who craved colors and light, find respite in that cave from the dun-colored world of the Depression, when waves of dirt billowed over their fields? Did she linger a moment longer before gathering the jars in her hands and walking back up the steps into the darkness of day?

When she spoke of the Depression, she talked of family gathered around the piano, prayers in the parlor, and the promise of better days. "I don't care what people say. The Depression wasn't that bad."

"Mother," I said, thinking of sepia photos of corn stubble in fields and shredded wood on buildings, "grasshoppers chewed up your corn and devoured the siding on outbuildings. You had no grass to feed cattle or rain for a garden. You were dirt poor."

"Oh for Heaven's sake, nobody had anything then," she said. "But we were happy. And we were always laughing."

She spoke seldom of the silt that seeped through slits in the walls, tiptoed around damp washcloths tucked in the window frames, and made a home in her lungs. Dust pneumonia, they called the fever, pain, and coughing spells that exhausted my teenage mother and left her lying in a hospital for weeks with a tube in her back to drain the muck from her lungs. Not until she stood naked in the dim light of a nursing home did I see the fleshy sinkhole between her ribs.

Fifty years ago, nearly fifty thousand women fished off Jeju, women who clung to gourds as they rested between dives, their linen gowns blossoming in the turquoise sea;

who during the war left the sea to put on trousers and fight the Japanese with knives and bare fists; who every day pass through the border between life and death when they swim to the ocean's floor.

Today that number has dwindled to six thousand. Educated by the money their mothers earned diving, many daughters of the sea women have rejected the dangerous life of fishing for careers in business and tourism. Perhaps the concierge at our hotel is this sea woman's daughter, a lovely woman with smooth skin and an impeccably tailored navy-blue blazer with a gold name tag pinned to her breast. "I can find you a seafood restaurant, or perhaps you'd like one that specializes in roasting the black pigs we raise on the island," she says as she fishes for our dinner reservations, her well-manicured fingers skimming over the computer's keyboard.

When I was a young woman, I saw my mother's face in the mirror one day—the face of the woman I didn't want to be whose work of laundry, cooking, and caring for children seemed mostly unsatisfying. When I strutted to campus in a business suit and pearls, I felt lucky, smug, that I had escaped the drudgery that I believed defined the women of my mother's generation. How long does it take for daughters to appreciate the choices their mothers made and their fortitude in coping with those they couldn't?

At dusk, as we drive back to the hotel, we pass several sea women standing in a circle in the middle of lava rocks. Some sort through tangled *mangsari* that trapped the octopus, mollusks, and *miyeok*, kelp, in its weave. Others dig egg-yolk flesh from abalone shells and sell it to tourists who swallow the flesh in one gulp and slurp the sea water from the shuck. In the way that women in my childhood shared the bounty of their harvests in jars of stewed tomatoes, beef, and jams, the sea women labor in communities called *eochongye*. They row out to the sea together, collectively clean the catches at the end of the day, and share the profits of the sea and of the soil they farm when they're not diving—garlic, green and yellow onions, and cabbage.

I turn around and look out the back window of the taxi, imagining the sea woman I'd spotted earlier is among those weathered faces, the salt-and-pepper hair plastered to their scalps, and biceps bulging against rubber sleeves. I want to think she is a *baeseonic*, a boat baby born when her mother took a break from gathering turban shells and delivered her daughter in a flood of blood and fluid that mingled with sea water in the boat. To imagine her as a little girl following her mother to the sea, frolicking in the waves with baby seals, and eating seagull eggs she found in nests along the shore.

Perhaps my sea woman will strip out of her wetsuit as some women do and stand naked on the rocks, scowling and shaking a finger at the tourists who stare. "*Weniriseyo?*" she might ask. "What's the matter?"

Later that night, my sea woman may gather around the flames of a *bulteok* to sing, "We are the poor, poor sea women of Jeju. . . my body has been tortured by the waves of sea." She may go home and collapse into bed with a crushing headache from the sea's pressure, waiting for the pillows of morphine to smother her. But for now, as the sun drops below the horizon and casts its light over the rocks, the ocean spray frames my sea woman in a shimmering halo like Sekhmet, the warrior goddess.

A circle of Irish women—my mother and my aunts— held mirrors in their hands as they watched my cousin Bobbie open a round, pewter-gray sample case of Beauty Counselor cosmetics. She held cardboard squares to their faces then consulted a color chart in her case. "Oh, pale linen is perfect for your skin color."

I have few memories of these women looking in mirrors. Many, I suspect, were uncomfortable, as I am, with what they saw—flat Irish faces, hooded eyes, and the hint of McManus jowls running beneath their chins. But mostly they had little time or money for vanity, with cooking, scrubbing mud off floors and flakes of manure from overalls, driving to town for machinery parts, and taking lunches to the fields.

Usually when these Irish women gathered, their laughter disturbed the silence of the farm so that even the grazing cattle lifted their heads. But that day they worked in silence. I sat in a corner, amazed to see these practical women stare in mirrors as they rubbed foundation over their faces with calloused fingers and pressed their lips together to seal the color in their lipstick. They patted their cheeks with powder puffs of cotton spun so finely I wanted to wrap my tongue around one, certain it tasted of sugar. The powder on their faces glistened like silt, and the room smelled of lavender and verbena.

The party ended when my mother sat at the piano, her fingers sailing over the keyboard. The women linked their arms around one another's waists and danced, their heads bobbing, their feet flashing as they sang, "Why don't you go where fashion sits? Puttin' on the Ritz." When sweat made tracks through the powder on their cheeks and their hair hung in limp strands on their necks, they packed their cosmetics into pewter-gray cases. "Can't believe I spent money for all this," one auntie said. "I don't think the cows will notice, and the husband certainly won't."

But Bobbie was the only entrepreneur among the women in the family, the first woman I knew to earn her own paycheck. Maybe out of blood loyalty they came to her party, perhaps sneaking coins from the cream and egg money they kept in jars in the pantry. Maybe it was the rare pleasure of pampering themselves that moved them to buy something as frivolous as makeup. Many women tucked the cases in the back of their closets and never opened them again.

Thousands of goddesses populate Jeju Island—goddesses of birth and death, of harvest and granaries, of kitchens and bathrooms. Their images are everywhere on the island—in paintings housed in museums and cultural centers, carved in smooth stone, and imagined in the clefts and nooks of the lava rocks that pepper the island. The *haenyeo* are living goddesses, their stories told in the chants of *simbang*, the shamans who perform the rituals to praise them and to appeal to the goddesses to protect them as they dive.

The most powerful goddess is Seolmundae Halmang, who birthed the island and is now grandmother to thousands of volcanic cones and humans. In one rock carving she is shown with a square face and loose skin draping beneath her eyes. Her rectangular mouth is a grin trapped in a sob like a sock-puppet monkey. Babies with aged faces and withered arms crawl over her naked body, their hands exploring her swollen belly, reaching like puppies for the nipples of her tubular breasts. She is a forceful female image embedded in the psyche of the islanders she has suckled for generations. There is something powerful in her nakedness, yet vulnerable in the way her eyes droop, the way her body slumps against the rock.

DaeSoon, the goddess of the moon, an eel-like creature covered in gold-and-red scales symbolized fertility. In an orange tunic and with a uterus-shaped headdress on her black hair, she floats among phallic-shaped flowers. She dictates women's blood cycles the way she controls the tides. For my mother and aunts, it was the rhythm of their blood cycle that controlled the nights they could lie with their husbands.

My Irish women birthed over forty babies among them. There was always the smell of curdled milk on their clothes and children wrapped around their legs as they worked in the kitchen. They diapered babies and dried tears with chapped hands, scolded children with weary eyes, and nursed them through bouts of measles and chickenpox. Yet they were merry storytellers, chortling when one aunt joked about living in a tarpaper shack with dirt floors. "I could never get the dirt off my girls' knees." They giggled when another spoke of paychecks too meager for children's shoes. "I stretched their old shoes and held them together with duct tape. My kids were so embarrassed, but their feet were covered."

When my mother and aunts gathered, we children understood without being told that our mothers' conversations were private, and we were to play softball until invited into the house. One day, I crept inside to use the bathroom and discovered a jellyfish of white satin floating in a sink of bloody water. I pinched the fabric between my fingertips and carefully lifted up a pair of panties. Although I rarely saw my prudish mother's underwear, I knew these were not hers. They were too small and too fancy with the ribbon of lace stitched to the waistband and legs.

Whose were they? What were they doing in that bloody pool? I tiptoed down the hallway and stood with my back against the wall, hoping to hear the woman who owned the panties confess she left them soaking in our sink. I heard one woman say, "I tell him over and over again that I can't. . ." But her voice grew so soft I couldn't hear the rest of the sentence. There were murmurs, low and indistinct. Then my mother said, "Oh, for cripes sakes, listen to us. It's not that bad. You can get used to anything."

I suspected there was a kinship between these women that had something to do with those ruby-tinted panties, maybe like the blood-sharing ceremony I once pretended to perform with my cousins when we colored red lines on our wrists and pressed our flesh together.

But this blood, I would one day learn, was something more intimate, an enduring blood thread that connects women. When my aunties left, I went back to the bathroom, but the jellyfish was gone and the sink was drained. I never told my mother of my discovery. I wonder now if the woman grieved when she felt those red blossoms unfolding beneath her. Or did she feel a guilty relief at the bleeding?

Death may come for the sea woman the day an abalone clamps its muscular leg on the knife strapped to her wrist and snares her to the stone. Or the day she lingers to grab one more clump of kelp or one more clam before frantically chasing the green stream of sun to the surface, her lungs bursting. Perhaps she will die in bed, exhausted and drugged as her daughters sing songs of lament.

In Mother's last days, she lay in Hospice, her legs swollen, her eyes closed, her hearing attuned to the voices of her children speaking softly of her life. "What a trickster," Kevin said. "Will you ever forget the time she mailed the green Jell-O with cottage cheese to our cousin Donald because he complained about eating it one Thanksgiving?"

"How did she cope with being widowed for over thirty years?" Jeanne asked. "Did you ever hear her complain about being lonely?"

"No," I said, "but I do remember the first Christmas Eve mass after Dad died. She slumped against me for just a moment when a tenor sang 'O Holy Night.' But then she straightened up and grinned and said, 'I just bout knocked you off the kneeler. That woulda been something.'"

We waited for the priest whose kindness and wisdom had guided us through Mother's many health crises and prepared us for her dying. But a new chaplain came into her room, a skinny, obsequious man with a stiff white collar who complained that his position was challenging and time-consuming. But he promised he would come back to pray with her. Although too weak to lift her head, she seemed somehow to rise from her bed and glare at him. She waved her skeletal fingers toward the door. "I wish you wouldn't." He read a psalm from his book and bolted. Six days later, she died without his prayers.

How should the daughters of such women mourn their passing?

Let me go to the cemetery as the sun unfolds its golden blanket over the prairie and spread a feast over my mother's grave—*stobhach gaelach*, with chunks of lamb and potato and turnips; soda bread with currants and caraway seed; piles of cabbage, apples, and cherries.

Let the sea women's daughters walk through fields of rapeseed and cover the rocks that pocket the shore with slices of *gyool*, little cakes of *bap*, shellfish, hard-boiled eggs, and a roasted pig, the smoke from incense curling through its snout.

Let me weave a Brigid's cross out of grasses and wheat and lay it on my mother's grave among shamrocks and wildflowers, and hang *clooties* of green linen on a scrubby cedar. Let my *caoineadh* be so fierce and mournful it invokes the spirit of Brigid, the sun goddess with vines and leaves woven in her hair whose keening shattered the silence of Celtic lands.

Let the shamanists dance on the black rocks, eyes glazed, snakes slithering around their arms, their swirling garments prisms in the sunlight. From her perch on Sunrise Peak, let the grandmother goddess weave grief and joy, birth and death, into a richly textured cloth, wrap it around the grieving daughters, and draw them to her breasts.

Let me write my mother's name in the dust on the black stone at her grave and watch as the wind carries it away to join the spirits of her ancestors who have become this land; let me know my mother in the sun that warms my back and in the fragrance of sage that perfumes her grave; let me hear her music in the wind that blows across the land.

Let the sea woman's daughters put her ashes in a *baetmujil* and sing rowing songs as Yeongdeung, the goddess of wind and sea, leads her paper boat away from the shore; let their keening drown out the crashing of waves and the shrieks of gulls as the boat begins its slow descent; let her become the kelp she once harvested and her ashes the grains of sand that shift with the tides.

And let her name be written on the rocks.

ABOUT THE AUTHOR

Mary Woster Haug grew up on the grasslands west of the Missouri River in South Dakota, the middle child of a Bohemian father, from whom she inherited her gypsy spirit, and an Irish mother, who offered the security of home. She writes about her childhood and the ways in which family, church, and land have shaped her.

This book began during her time as an exchange professor at Chungnam National University in Daejeon, South Korea. That experience sparked memories of South Dakota. When she witnessed an ancestor veneration ceremony, she remembered a prairie cemetery near her childhood farm; at the public baths she recalled her mother naked and shivering in a nursing home; standing at the DMZ she brought back a pond in a patch of grassland now plowed and planted with sorghum.

She has been published in national and regional anthologies as well as literary journals and news magazines. Her essay about visiting the Korean baths was nominated for a Pushcart Prize. She edited *The Woster Brothers' Brand,* a collection of her brothers' columns published in South Dakota daily newspapers and agricultural journals.

Mary taught English for thirty years at South Dakota State University. When she retired she lived in The Badlands National Park in Interior, South Dakota, for five weeks, serving as a writer-in-residence.

She and her husband, Ken, live in Brookings, South Dakota. They have a daughter, Maura, who lives in Minneapolis with her husband, Steve, and children, Casey and Molly.

RECENT BOOKS BY BOTTOM DOG PRESS

BOOKS IN THE HARMONY SERIES
Daughters of the Grasslands: Memoir
By Mary Woster Haug, 198 pgs. $18
Gifted and Talented: A Novel
By Julia Watts, 202 pgs. $18
Lake Winds: Poems
By Larry Smith, 220 pgs. $18
Echo: Poems
By Christina Lovin, 114 pgs. $16
Stolen Child: A Novel
By Suzanne Kelly, 338 pgs. $18
The Canary: A Novel
By Michael Loyd Gray, 196 pgs. $18
On the Flyleaf: Poems
By Herbert Woodward Martin, 106 pgs. $16
The Harmonist at Nightfall: Poems of Indiana
By Shari Wagner, 114 pgs. $16
Painting Bridges: A Novel
By Patricia Averbach, 234 pgs. $18
Ariadne & Other Poems
By Ingrid Swanberg, 120 pgs. $16
The Search for the Reason Why: New and Selected Poems
By Tom Kryss, 192 pgs. $16
Kenneth Patchen: Rebel Poet in America
By Larry Smith, Revised 2nd Edition, 326 pgs. Cloth $28
Selected Correspondence of Kenneth Patchen,
Edited with intro by Allen Frost, Paper $18/ Cloth $28
Awash with Roses: Collected Love Poems of Kenneth Patchen
Eds. Laura Smith and Larry Smith
With introduction by Larry Smith, 200 pgs. $16

HARMONY COLLECTIONS AND ANTHOLOGIES
d.a.levy and the mimeograph revolution
Eds. Ingrid Swanberg and Larry Smith, 276 pgs. $20
Come Together: Imagine Peace
Eds. Ann Smith, Larry Smith, Philip Metres, 204 pgs. $16
Evensong: Contemporary American Poets on Spirituality
Eds. Gerry LaFemina and Chad Prevost, 240 pgs. $16
America Zen: A Gathering of Poets
Eds. Ray McNiece and Larry Smith, 224 pgs. $16
Family Matters: Poems of Our Families
Eds. Ann Smith and Larry Smith, 232 pgs. $16

Recent Books by Bottom Dog Press

CPSIA information can be obtained at www.ICGtesting.com
Printed in the USA
LVOW06s1055250814

400782LV00001B/160/P